Confident Entertaining

Confident Entertaining

Carolyn Shealy Self

sketches by Doty Lovett

THOMAS NELSON INC., PUBLISHERS
Nashville   New York

First edition

Library of Congress Cataloging in Publication Data

Self, Carolyn.
  Confident entertaining.

  Includes indes.
  1. Entertaining.   2. Menus.   3. Cookery.   I. Title.
TX731.S44   642'41   76–41764
ISBN 0–8407–4055–7

For Bill

1931049

In Appreciation

I want to express my deep appreciation to Dorothy Reeves, Mary Ringle, Zonetta Lee, and Shirley Gantt. Without Dorothy, Mary and Zonetta to do the typing, there would be no book. Shirley is my proofreader, making sure that my sentences have a matching noun and verb!

My family has been patient in enduring late dinners and my more-than-normal absentmindedness. You are appreciated!

I am grateful for all my friends who have so graciously helped with flowers, food, and hard work at parsonage parties through the years.

To the consultants, the contributors of ideas and recipes—a great big thank you for helping me make this book possible.

Consultants

Frances Moore is the wife of John L. Moore, Jr., who is Assistant to the Vice President in charge of marketing for The Simmons Company. Frances learned the secrets of entertaining elegantly in a small New York apartment. They now live in a lovely apartment in Atlanta.

Isobel Leonard Spearman (Mrs. Bonner) has been an authority on flower arrangement for over twenty-five years. Her home and garden reflect her expertise and love of beautiful surroundings.

Betty Van Gerpen is the wife of Atlanta attorney Earl Van Gerpen. Betty has an inborn flair for giving exciting parties and making her guests feel special.

Lealice Dehoney is the wife of Dr. Wayne Dehoney who is pastor of the Walnut Street Baptist Church, Louisville, Kentucky. Lealice is President of the Women's Missionary Union of Kentucky. She brings warmth and hospitality to any situation.

Cascile Knight is the wife of Dr. Malcolm Knight who is pastor of the Southside Baptist Church, Jacksonville, Florida. Cascile is a gracious and charming hostess with the ability to cope with any situation.

Roy and Nanci Simmons entertain weekly (sometimes more often) in their home as part of Roy's position as Manager of Community/Customer Relations in the Public Relations Department of Lockheed, Georgia Company. This is a successful team effort.

Bill and Norma Key also find entertaining in their home a gracious way of enhancing Bill's position with Lockheed as Director of Industrial Relations. Here is another example of teamwork.

Lou Lolley is the wife of Dr. Randall Lolley who is President of Southeastern Baptist Theological Seminary, Wake Forest, North Carolina. Lou is remarkable in her ability to meet protocol requirements and at the same time make her guests feel warm and comfortable.

Ella Moore is the wife of Atlanta businessman John B. Moore. Their authentic Williamsburg home is the setting for many lovely parties. It is a joy to be a guest in their home.

Wynelle MacMullen is an elementary school librarian in Ocala, Florida. She is living proof that you can have a successful "spur of the moment party" even with her four-year-old grandson on the loose in her small apartment. Wynelle also is representative of those who live alone and entertain frequently.

Doty Bean is the wife of Maurice D. Bean who is Chargé d'Affaires, United States Embassy, Monrovia, Liberia. Included in Maurice's proposal of marriage to Doty were these questions: Do you like to travel? Do you like people? Do you like an active social life? Little did she know it would require almost twenty-four hours daily entertaining duties. Her motto is "Keep smiling."

Anne King is the wife of Dr. William B. King. Anne collected and coordinated the material from Thomasville friends. The love Anne and Bill have for people is reflected in every area of their life. They are representative of the true gracious Southern hospitality for which Thomasville, Georgia, is famous.

Acknowledgements

Mrs. John Barrington, Hostess, Wieuca Road Baptist Church, Atlanta, Georgia. Mrs. Matthew Spearman, Atlanta, Georgia. Mr. Charles Wood, Director of Food Services for Sky Valley Resort, Dillard, Georgia.

From Thomasville, Georgia: Mrs. Isobel Donaldson (Garden Center); Mrs. Paul Hjort; Mrs. Jack Kelly; Mrs. Talbot Nunnally, III; Mrs. Rudolph Davis; Mrs. W. R. Thomas, Jr.; Mrs. Huddie Cheney; Mrs. Tom Vann, Jr.; Mrs. James R. Neill; Mrs. Clifford Campbell; Mrs. Paul J. McCollum.

From Atlanta, Georgia: Mrs. Henry Holley whose husband is the coordinator of Billy Graham Crusades Overseas; Mrs. Stephen S. P. Chen, wife of Consulate General, Republic of China; Dr. Rosaio An, Professor of Political Science, Atlanta University, who with her husband, Dr. Nack Young An, entertains frequently for the Korean community; and Mrs. Walter Bunzl, Chancellor for the Consulate of Austria.

Contents

Preface

This is a collection of thoughts, hints, and general hodgepodge of information designed to be helpful to both the novice and the experienced hostess. Hopefully, it will give confidence to the amateur and guide the most uncoordinated, unorganized, witless one through the murky waters of punch, coffee, and tea.

Surely every bride has had the first party or first company dinner jitters. This is compounded if you're in a new town and you're entertaining your husband's business colleagues and/or their wives. It's fun at first when you're the new arrival and there's a whirl of parties in your honor. Then one morning you wake up with a black cloud hovering over your left shoulder, and you know the time of reciprocation has arrived. There are several ways to handle this. You could go back to bed, but this will only result in spreading the black cloud disease to your right shoulder. Another way is to avoid appearing in public and have the telephone disconnected. This would be difficult to explain to your husband and next to impossible to pull off. So—pour yourself another cup of coffee, find a pencil and piece of paper, and start planning.

I am writing this as a minister's wife who has poured countless cups of coffee for young and old, rich and poor, and all those in between. No matter who you are, whether you are the wife of a businessman, mechanic, doctor, professor, minister, or congressman, or if you are single, remember that when you extend an invitation to someone, you are offering yourself to them. An invitation into your home or apartment is an invitation into *you*. When you think of entertaining in this way, it puts things in their proper order. It makes the hostess the most important ingredient in a successful party—however large or small. My definition of a successful party is not how beautiful the flowers, delicious the food, or perfect the table setting, but whether or not there is a nice comfortable warm glow that permeates each guest.

Confident Entertaining

What Is a Party?

Entertaining, large or small, is like being the star of your own play, your home being a "theater in the round." It can be a brilliant, sparkling, star-studded success, or it can fizzle flat along with the ginger ale that was left over in the punch bowl. Just as the success of a play to a large measure depends on the compatibility and effort of the actors and audience, so the success or failure of a party depends on the hostess and/or host and the guests.

There are certain people who are so pleasant and exude such personal warmth and charm that their friends anxiously await their next party and are crushed if they have a conflict and have to decline. You, too, can have this reputation with just a little planning, the proper attitude, and (hopefully) the cooperation of the household.

Betty Van Gerpen says that to receive friends in an atmosphere that is warm, friendly, refined, and gracious is possible only if you express warmth, friendliness, refinement, and graciousness in your daily life—week after week, year after year.

Without exception everyone interviewed agreed it is most important to relax and be yourself. Guests reflect the attitude of the host and hostess, and if you've just had a grim disagreement or start apologizing for the condition of the house or food, everyone will be depressed and exhausted long before the evening is over. Roy and Nanci Simmons entertain people from all over the world more frequently than I like to think about. Roy was sincere when he said to me, "It's always a pleasure to have people in our home. We don't invite people unless we're going to enjoy the evening also. We're not out to impress anybody but just to have an evening of good fun and fellowship."

Parties don't "just happen"—at least most of them don't. There are things to do and not to do. Your first party is always the hardest, whether it's your first party ever or first in a new city. You'll be a little uptight, so make it simple, write down your plans, organize, and then relax and enjoy!

Guests should be made to feel very special from the moment they ring the doorbell. The host and hostess should be dressed and ready to greet guests at least half an hour before the appointed time. Greet them with enthusiasm and be aware of something complimentary to say to each one. "You look so lovely tonight." "That color is so becoming to you." "We have looked forward to having you in our home." "I'm anxious for my friends to meet you." Try to be at the door to greet each person, then introduce him/her to the others and tell something interesting about him. For instance, "Tom Smith, I want you to meet Jack Jones. He's a great golfer." Or, "Nancy and Mike, meet Al and Mary. They have three boys, too." Or, "Betty, Louise is an avid needlepointer, also."

The guests bring some responsibility with them to be charming and agreeable, but there are some people who are painfully bashful and probably have to muster all their courage to make it through the door and mumble hello. Here is where the discerning hostess can guide the bashful one into the circle of casual chitchat. Hopefully, other guests will be helpful. The hostess should keep her eyes and ears open and the conversation pleasant. Try to give each person an opportunity to participate in the conversation. If, at the dinner table, one guest dominates and becomes boring, be ready to change the subject gracefully and shift the attention to someone else.

Unless there is a specific reason for it (like a Super Bowl TV party), parties are more enjoyable if you can keep the males and females together. If the men need to talk business, they should have a business luncheon, and if the women want to discuss child care or physical ailments, they can do it at a morning coffee. Of course, there will be several conversational groups during the evening consisting of all men or all women, but these should not be long-lasting group sessions. It takes practice and sensitivity to maintain your spot in the "director's chair" and make your actors (the guests) smashing sensations. You'll get rave reviews if you can avoid scene stealing by someone who has a loud or whiney voice getting into a political, religious, or personal harangue.

The guest has a responsibility in responding quickly to an invitation. If it is a dinner party, the hostess needs to know whether or not to invite someone else. It is just a courtesy that should not be overlooked to let your hostess know your plans. If you happen to be the hostess and you haven't heard and you're rapidly reaching the panic stage, you may very tactfully call the delinquent guest, saying something like this: "I do hope you received the invitation and will be able to come to the party (dinner, whatever). I have been out so much that I was afraid I missed your call." If they decline, you can say, "Oh, we had hoped you could come. You would have made the evening special." Or, if they accept, say, "Oh, how wonderful. You will make the party so special." This should not sound insincere because each person does have something special to add to a gathering. Calling is a good way to find out if they plan to come. Let's face it, sometimes a forgetful husband may carry letters around in his pocket for days, so don't waste ugly thoughts on seemingly thoughtless people. Most of us live in the midst of a whirlwind, and a family crisis may erase the thoughts of a party or appointment temporarily.

I'm being very kind about this because I was guilty not long ago of forgetting an after-church birthday party for a good friend. I had accepted enthusiastically because it would be an interesting, happy group of friends. Sundays for us are generally a marathon of activity that would challenge the healthiest person. There is the responsibility felt for the physical comfort and spiritual and emotional well-being of forty-five hundred people for three worship services, plus Church School and other activities, the feeding of a family and any friends who may float through, etc., etc., in all a pretty draining day. Well, it was an especially hectic Sunday and I completely forgot my friend's party. *What* could I say? No excuse in the world would be acceptable. So I just called and told the truth, and I was so relieved to feel the warm, understanding vibrations coming through. Those friends are even more special to me now because they accepted my apology and still love me. I said all this to point out that we're all capable of mistakes, but there is usually a good reason, and you may be able to sense that your negligent friend needs you to listen and extend warmth and encouragement.

One of my friends who has made an art of being both hostess and guest offers this suggestion very strongly. If you are on a special diet for medical reasons and are invited to a dinner party, say something like this: "We would love to come, but I have to have special food and it would be too much trouble for you. Please include us another time and perhaps I'll be over this problem." This gives the hostess the opportunity to say how disappointed she is and perhaps she'll include you in another type of party soon. It puts a damper on the dinner if one person refuses (for any reason) to eat the food that has been prepared. Or perhaps the special diet (such as low sodium) could be adhered to without very much trouble and served discreetly to avoid attention or comments. If you are on a diet for weight control, cut down on calorie intake before and after the party. This applies to both guest and hostess. Smaller portions can be taken but try some of everything. In deference to finicky eaters, a hostess should avoid serving any food that may be truly offensive.

Sometimes the most fun parties are impromptu. Invite some friends over after church or school or meeting. Always try to keep a pound cake or something in the freezer that you can pull out and run in the oven for a few minutes. Cake and coffee or hot chocolate are super, or soup and a sandwich. Or scrambled eggs and toast around the kitchen table make a cozy, friendly atmosphere.

I really don't know where this fits in, but it is another area of awareness in knowing when to ask for help (hostess) and when to give it (guest). Have you ever been to a dinner party where the hostess and the women guests jumped up to clear the table? The confusion is unbearable and the guests are not that much help. The host may discreetly help in clearing the table, but if he is all thumbs or there is no host, a guest who is a close friend should be asked (ahead of time) to help if the hostess really feels that she needs it.

When a hostess says to leave the dishes, she means it. It is easier to clean up in a leisurely, organized way after the last guest has departed. If you are the hostess, it is great if your husband can pitch in and help. If he does, be sure to brag about him. However, be patient if he just can't do anything more constructive than worry and wring his hands. You can figure out ways to compensate for lack of help. The best thing he can do anyway is to be in an expansive (and expensive!) mood and sensitive to the "feeling" of the group. If you are single, you need not feel "out of it." It's your attitude that makes the difference, not whether or not you have a joint venture.

One more important suggestion. I feel very strongly about this, and almost all the contributors mentioned it. As host/hostess you set the tone of the party. It is your home, so be yourself. If it is your custom to have a blessing before dinner, do not hesitate to do so. We always hold hands around the table and Bill thanks God for friends and asks a special blessing on each family represented. If you would like to do this, say something like, "We always hold hands around the table and ask God to bless our friends," and you extend your hands, bow your head, and either you or the host ask a *brief* blessing. This horizontal, vertical touching may be more meaningful to your guests than any food or words the rest of the evening.

Whether you're the hostess or the guest, you have a responsibility to carry out your role with charm and grace. After one of our parties, large or small, simple or elaborate, well planned or impromptu, we invariably ask ourselves, "Was it a good party?" Listen to what veteran party givers Norma and Bill Key say: "After the party is over—how do you know if it was a good party? Did your guests enjoy it? Was it successful? The acid test, almost one hundred percent accurate, can be obtained by answering one question: 'Did *I* enjoy it; did *I* have a good time?' If your answer is yes, then wonder no more—the guests did, too!"

But, Mother,
What About Me?
And the Dog . . .
And the Cat?

Children and pets are "extras" who are born scene stealers. They sometimes add a touch of drama that borders on hysteria. I'll never forget my ordeal with the frogs and the missionary society meeting. When our sons were about two and four, the older wandered through the kitchen where I was sliding the coffee cake into the oven, and I asked, "What are you looking for, Lee?" His reply produced instant knots in the pit of my stomach. "Bryan and I dropped our frogs and they're lost!" This was about forty-five minutes before the meeting was to start—hardly enough time to round up frogs. Believe me, they aren't easy to catch inside the house! Fortunately, the baby-sitter arrived and saved the day. Can't you just see a frog hopping out from the corner during a solemn moment?

Unless it is specifically a family occasion, everyone will appreciate the absence of children. If your children are too young to entertain themselves and go on to bed, you should include the cost of a baby-sitter when you plan your party. If your guests are paying for a sitter for their children, they are not anxious to have yours dominate the evening. It really puts too much responsibility on the child for him to be allowed to assume the "starring" role. He isn't experienced enough to curb his exhibition instincts. Depending on the age and temperament of the child, his appearance on the stage should be supported by his mother and father and he should be exited quietly and quickly.

The very nicest solution, if it is possible, is to arrange an overnight visit with grandparents. This way you get to sleep late the next morning, and it's a nice change for everybody. I really do love children, but let's face it, they are all-consuming. We all need a chance to eat without having to jump up to mop spilled milk, a chance to complete a sentence without being interrupted.

Pets look dimly on the prospect of a party. Like children, they are aware of your first thoughts about the production and become very grumpy and nervous. Always have handy some instant rug cleaner or spot remover and check the party rooms at the last minute. Animals have an uncanny way of going where they shouldn't when you least expect it. Do lock them in another part of the house or outside—you may have a guest who is highly allergic to dogs or cats. Your cat or dog may sulk, but maybe a nice bowl of tuna or a juicy bone will put you back in his good graces.

Nanci and Roy Simmons have four dogs—three poodles and a Labrador—that are well behaved and like to meet people. They are left in the backyard unless the deck will be used for the party. In that case they are put in the garage with the car door open. They sit patiently in the car, not even barking, thinking they are going somewhere. The dogs are well trained, Roy says, because he brings them in sometime during the evening and lets them sit up and shake hands for everybody and then make their exit. This story has been a source of amusement to me ever since I heard it. I can just imagine those dogs sitting in the car waiting for the chauffeur. I probably shouldn't tell you about the dogs and cats we have had at our house, but I will. One evening before an Open House we were giving for the church, the dog chased the cat up the Christmas tree, and the tree, decorations, and cat fell over in the middle of the floor. Now that would cause panic in the heart of *any* hostess. We also had a cat that claimed a certain chair in the family room. It was not unusual for the cat to come in, find an unsuspecting guest sitting there, and sit and meow and pace around until we put either the guest or the cat out!

Children who grow up in an active household with entertaining being the normal way of life find it the natural thing to do as an adult and on their own. My parents had a lot of company—we had a lot of family and friends drop by for dinner or dessert, and it was natural for me, when I was old enough, to be the helper. This was good training for me, and I would certainly encourage any mother of daughters to take advantage of this opportunity, not only to teach but gain needed help. All the contributors who have daughters agree that depending on their age, stage of coordination, and disposition, they can be a delightful source of help. However, if your patience is short or your temperament clashes with your daughter, you'll both be losers, so just don't demand or expect more than can be gracefully given. Having two sons (who are basically male chauvinists), I can only hope that they will be polite and charming. I can also expect to get the garage and walk swept and unkind remarks about the small sandwiches. I learned the hard way to either hide or place threatening "Do Not Disburb" signs on all party cakes and cookies.

It is nice to have older children help greet guests, help with the coats, pass food for a few minutes, and then excuse themselves. Sometimes it is nice to let them have their snacks and a TV in one of the bedrooms if you do not have a separate playroom. It is best to feed them early—either some of your dinner or their favorite "carry out" food (hamburgers, chicken, etc.). Norma Key says that sometimes after a coffee she sets up the leftover food just like it was for her party and lets the children invite their friends. She says their manners are beautiful and they enjoy the attention.

Cascile and Malcolm Knight have three lovely daughters (all now married) who still remember the very special dinner party in honor of the new hospital administrator and his wife. Gwen, the oldest, and Anne, the youngest, were certain they could serve the vegetables and pour the coffee, but they weren't so sure about Judy keeping her mind on her business. They decided that serving the rolls was the least hazardous job of all and surely Judy could handle that. It is still a family joke that the rolls landed in the lap of the guest of honor!

Many times there are dishes that your teen-agers can prepare for you. Lealice Dehoney says that their daughters, Kathy and

Becky (now grown), began to help with preparation and serving when they were about nine or ten years old. Betty Van Gerpen's daughter (age thirteen) is an expert crepe maker. So since experience is the best teacher, I think that creative entertaining is natural to those reared in that atmosphere. But, never fear, no matter what your background, you too can be a charming hostess.

What about children and pets and entertaining?

1. If your children are small, get a baby-sitter. Serve the guests a late dinner after the children are tucked in for *sure*. Keep it simple. This means limiting your company to one or two couples and serving food that needs no last-minute care.

2. Until your children are old enough to take care of themselves and go on to bed, get a sitter so you can enjoy your own guests.

3. As they get older, let them help in small ways and then exit. Do not expect miracles.

4. Don't be upset if you can't get complete cooperation. Make adjustments, but don't allow yourself to be manipulated by your children.

5. Occasionally have small parties that include your children's friends (and/or your friends' children).

6. Pets are best kept away from the party area—however you can accomplish it!

How to Avoid Bankruptcy

The lack of money may or may not be your problem. Even affluent people usually do not like to spend money needlessly, so a household budget is always a good idea. Sometimes that's all it is—an idea—but if you are really concerned about keeping your bank account in respectable condition, some bookkeeping and plans have to be made. Neither my husband nor I enjoy this. We are not very well educated mathematically and we do a lot of moaning and groaning. It's just one of those chores that go along with living.

If you plan to have a party, you really need to sit down and decide how much you can spend. If you plan ahead, you can have several weeks to watch for food bargains and prepare a few more budget meals for the family in order to have a little extra to spend for the party. There's no way you can entertain without it costing you something extra. (Unless somebody gives you a cake, and you just have a cake and coffee party—and that's nice, too!) Having a household budget and keeping good records on expenses helps when income tax time rolls around. Don't forget that if you are entertaining for business purposes, you can deduct these expenses only if you have accurate records. Keep all grocery checks and cash register receipts. Keep records of all your expenses such as cost of a maid (if you have one especially for the occasion), candles, invitations, flowers, etc. You should also keep a record of who was there so that the cost won't be out of proportion to how many you entertained and what you served, whether it was a dinner, coffee, or brunch.

When you are having dinner for your husband's boss, be sure you think about the menu from all angles. If you blow the whole month's budget on prime rib or filet mignon, the boss may think one of two things: (1) he's paying your husband too much if you can afford that, or (2) you have questionable reasoning powers. For less money you can make a delicious oven roast cooked in mushroom soup. Sliced thin and served with wild rice, it tastes like beef stroganoff and it's easy to fix!

Don't wait till you can afford something like prime rib. Fellowship is more important than food, and there's no limit on the fun good friends can have. If you have a spaghetti budget, then by all means have spaghetti—but with a flair. Use a checkered tablecloth or place mats or maybe plain place mats with checkered napkins. Use lots of middle-height candles, stand some long (uncooked) spaghetti in a pottery or glass pitcher or anything you may have, add a decorated wooden spatula, turn down the lights, turn on the music, and there you are! It is nice to forewarn your guests when you invite them by saying: "We're having a spaghetti supper and would love for you to come." "Supper" lets them know it won't be formal! You can wear a long cotton skirt and feel very festive. It depends on your attitude, not your budget!

It would be great to develop a specialty over the years like a really super spaghetti sauce, chili, a chicken and rice dish, an unusual dressing for tossed salad, or homemade rolls or biscuits. I think that homemade rolls, cinnamon rolls, or biscuits make *anything* (even leftover leftovers!) taste good. They're easy to make with a little practice, I promise.

Cascile Knight, Nanci Simmons, and Mrs. Bunzl use round tops cut from masonite or plywood to be used on card tables to seat six people. The Simmonses have one that seats eight. The tops (to seat six) can be cut from two sheets of four-feet-by-eight-feet masonite. For ease in storing, the tops can be cut in half and hinged on the side that is placed on the card table. You can make cloths from remnants and mill ends; a queen-sized sheet will make a floor-length cloth. The variety in types of cloths (always no-iron!) is endless. Napkins made to match or contrast add a special touch. No-iron fabric makes laundering a breeze. Think of that spaghetti supper on a round table placed in front of a cozy fire on a winter's night—or on the patio or porch on a mild spring evening! I am definitely going to acquire a tabletop or two. Mrs. Bunzl adds that these tops can be purchased in one of our Atlanta department stores. This would take the place of the dining-room table until you find and can afford just what you want, and it will always be useful.

Remember that whatever you purchase or make is going to be used over and over, so take time to think through all color schemes, making sure that you do not impulsively buy something that will eventually be buried in the back corner of your storage closet.

Decide early what you want to collect (pitchers of crystal or pottery, figurines, bells, shells, teapots, demitasse sets, whatever your interest is) and let your family and friends know for birthday and Christmas gifts. Experiment with ways to use these in decorating your table, and you can have interesting and inexpensive centerpieces.

If you were not fortunate enough to receive a silver tea service for a wedding gift (or if you aren't married), you should definitely start a silver savings fund. Don't worry about keeping silver polished. Silver now doesn't require polishing as often, and there are excellent polishes available that are also protective and tarnish resistant. Silver is an investment (should be insured and engraved on bottom) and will be a family treasure. I also like pewter. Every home should have at least one beautiful treasure because it impresses the children and sets a tone they should inherit from you.

I have asked many people what they consider their most valuable entertaining "equipment" or what every hostess should have, and here are the results. They are not in any order. You have to decide which you need most or can afford first, or which suits your style of entertaining.

1. A *silver service* and a *punch bowl and cups* receive top and equal billing. The punch bowl can be silver or crystal. Silver is always so elegant. We were given a lovely crystal punch bowl (two, in fact) and one hundred cups, and it is so nice not to have to round up extra cups. I enjoy using our silver service in the dining room and the punch bowl in the family room. However, if you have a dining table long enough and a large room, you can certainly use the silver service and the punch bowl at either end (and it's all right to mix silver and crystal).

2. *Silver trays* or *crystal trays.* Keep the silver trays stored in silver cloth or heavy plastic—not plastic wrap.

3. Everybody should have at least one pair of *candlesticks.* A collection of candlesticks can be *so* versatile. *Please* do not use candles before six o'clock unless it's a wedding!

4. A *silver epergne* offers many possibilities as does a *crystal cornucopia.* Mrs. Bonner Spearman suggests using fruit and flowers. Examples: a crystal cornucopia pouring to the center of the table with fresh peaches, the centerpiece of creamy peach dahlias in the same shades placed on a pale green linen cloth; yellow spider chrysanthemums arranged with green grapes cascading from the container with two smaller arrangements of lemons and grapes on either side; and for the truly stunning (and expensive, unless you grow tulips) white tulips with black throats in the silver epergne and black olives in the four little vases! Mrs. Spearman also suggests using pink and lavender tulips in the silver epergne and candy to match in the four little vases. Or try fruit in the large epergne carrying out a color scheme with small flowers in the same shades in the four little vases.

5. For a spectacular addition consider a *silver candelabrum.* It is elegant to use on the buffet with candles reflected in a mirror. You can also use it as an epergne by adding glass epergnes (I have some six inches and some four inches in diameter).

6. My favorite serving piece is a hand-painted china *soup tureen.* The little "off the beaten path" inns in Germany and Switzerland serve such delicious soup from lovely tureens. I hinted to my artist mother and *voilà*—a beautiful soup tureen with matching candlesticks. The tureen is just the right size for many uses. When not being used for soup or stew, it is gorgeous in the fall with chrysanthemums (any color) for a centerpiece—very informal. Also it is just the right size for a five-inch pot of blooming begonias, geraniums, a pretty fern, baby tears, leaves from your shrubs, or whatever you have or can buy or borrow. In fact, any pretty serving container will do for this and a nice ceramic flowerpot would be a good investment.

7. A *hurricane lamp* placed over a low brass, crystal, or silver candle holder (depending on where you use it) is good to withstand air-conditioning drafts or the breeze on a patio—and especially lovely for Williamsburg or colonial settings. These can be quite simple and inexpensive or very elaborate with beautiful etching.

8. A *crystal bowl* for summer arrangements of wild ferns is on my want list. That with white organdy mats (if you're extra smart, appliqué in ferns) and crystal candle holders would be so cool and fresh.

9. Don't forget to give serious thought to your selections of *glass, china, silver, linens,* and *accessories.* There should be a relationship in all these for a formal or informal table. Remember to consider the dining room walls, draperies, and rug and whether or not you have a period room, such as French or Victorian. Many corporate migrants have to move a number of times and don't have the opportunity to stay in one home forever. This makes it doubly important to make good basic selections in the personal items you pack so carefully at moving time. "Things" and furniture are important to the whole family. We moved when our boys were about two and one-half years old and one year old. Lee, the older, toured the new house and checked each room to see if all our familiar things were there and then said, "It's okay, Bryan. Everything's here."

10. A *tea cart*—antique or otherwise. It does not have to be expensive. Sometimes at a larger dinner party, it is nice to have one by the host and one by the hostess.

Here are some random ideas that I don't know where else to put:

1. Norma Key has collected seashells through the years and uses them in either a silver footed tray or cut-glass bowl—with candles it is stunning. She also has shell napkin rings.

2. At a sit-down dinner the centerpiece should not be over fourteen inches in height.

3. Try these—one rose bud with ivy; small basket of violets;

floating camellias; azalea blooms; a pot of hyacinths or tulips; and at Christmastime, a big silver (or crystal) bowl filled with holly berries and six red carnations.

4. Mr. Charles Wood cuts down a pumpkin about one-third from the top in sawtooth design, scrapes it out very clean, then pours melted paraffin wax in and rolls it around to coat the inside well, and sprays the pumpkin with a light coat of clear shellac. When dry, a container of fall flowers or a dried arrangement set in this will last for weeks, maybe months!

5. Magnolia leaves are beautiful natural or sprayed silver or gold at Christmas—also pinecones.

6. Take to the woods and fields. Keep your eyes open for unusual rocks, driftwood, a two- or three-inch cross section of a log (follow the tree surgeons!); many seedpods, grasses, and weeds dry nicely for longer-lasting arrangements. My mother and I nearly got bogged down in the Okefenokee Swamp getting just "one more" cattail!

7. Daisies are always pretty and inexpensive to add to yard greenery.

8. If you are a gardener, you have it *made*! Encourage your husband to grow roses (or *anything*) for therapy. This is a good outdoor activity for him, and he'll enjoy getting the raves from your guests. If he isn't so inclined, then it is up to you. It is also good therapy for you if you have patience. I'm afraid that house-plants, marigolds, daisies, begonias, and geraniums respond to my spasmodic gardening attempts best. If you are far enough south, camellias and gardenias require almost no care—just be careful about putting any odoriferous flowers such as gardenias or Easter lilies in the house. I have instant allergy and can't breathe!

9. Find a wholesale nursery and make friends with the owner or manager. He will usually be happy to sell you plants that he has left over at less than half the retail price. I have gotten absolutely gorgeous potted begonias for a centerpiece for about $1.50 each. I can usually keep them blooming for ages with liquid fertilizer. I then root the cuttings.

10. Whenever you are near a wholesale fabric store or there's a *good* sale anywhere on fabric, go and browse around with an eye for your colors (checked gingham, prints, florals, solids) in no-iron cotton suitable for tablecloths, place mats, napkins, basket liners for picnics, table runners, whatever. Anybody can put a hem in place mats or napkins, or can apply a lace edge (also no-iron). You don't have to use it right away. Keep a drawer or box under the bed for fabric goodies—also a pair of pinking shears in case you're in a hurry. Keep the shears in the box also or you'll never see them again. The scissors gobbler will hide them! A bias strip of checked gingham makes a darling tie for a basket of daisies. Line your breadbaskets. Wrap and tape on floral sticks and add to pot plants or an all-green centerpiece —use your imagination. Yarn in various colors is handy to have on hand.

11. If you ever find a well-preserved bird's nest, you'll have a treasure. Look for a nicely shaped branch of something with lots of limbs (low), place the branch in styrofoam with the nest in a suitable limb. Use blue marbles or something similar and may-be you can find an inexpensive ceramic bird the right size at an import bazaar. Place pine straw, leaves, pine nuggets or moss around the base to hide the styrofoam and there you are— a nature lover's delight!

12. There are still people who have guinea fowl and peacocks, and you could beg or buy a few feathers to add to a design.

13. A Christmas tree should reflect the personality of your family. Collect special balls and ornaments that are meaningful to your family. If you are single, you can probably afford a few lovely expensive ornaments to cherish. Don't fail to put the handmade decorations of the children in a prominent place on the tree and preserve them carefully through the years. Half of the fun of Christmas is digging through the boxes and coming up with a treasure. "I made this!" Building memories is what it's all about, whether it's family, friends, or total strangers when you're setting the stage and directing the action. Don't be inhibited by what someone may think. It's the feeling they carry away that is important.

I don't know why I put that in about Christmas trees except that I have had ambivalent feelings about it myself. I have often thought, "Now, next year we'll have a tree with all gold ornaments and ribbons," or some such, and then I know I couldn't carry that off. It wouldn't be us—we're sort of hodgepodge with the ornaments (dating from my childhood) and the lights are unmentionable. First of all, it takes a full forty-eight hours to untangle them, another two hours to find the right combination of extension cords, and at least four people to take turns giving instructions! I promise you that I always (well, almost always) put the lights away very carefully so that we'll avoid this crisis, but sometime during the summer the winter gremlins get restless and entertain themselves in our attic with this jumbling activity and do they have fun!

Also we have a yard full of living Christmas trees—a good idea if you need trees! Buy them early—they are cheaper and prettier.

How to avoid bankruptcy? We'll talk about food and menus later, but basically it's a matter of being unafraid to come to grips with the reality of money in all areas of living.

1. Don't impulsively buy an expensive item. Think about where you will put it and what you will use it for, and how often. Don't buy something just because you think you have to have it to make an impression—it will be your budget that will suffer depression.

2. Develop the imagination that's lurking down there in your being. Explore your yard, the woods, seashore, mountains, whatever is around you for interesting items.

3. Buy small house plants from the department store (under $1.00 usually and watch for sales) and pot them yourself. Hanging baskets and greenery at strategic places add so much charm and reflect your care about your home. Use liquid fertilizer and speak kindly!

4. A room waiting for furniture can be the best place for a basket picnic supper or lunch, or a stand up hors d'oeuvre and punch or coffee party. Use card tables for food service. In other words, don't apologize for no furniture—suit your style to your situation.

5. There is no limit on your warmth and friendliness and this will make the difference in a good party—not how much money you spend.

What Do I Do, and When? Organize!

1931049

I've always had an aversion to lists and charts and files, but with great reluctance I'm here to admit that I wish I had some and I promise to do better! I was very fortunate to have been given the responsibility of planning, shopping for, and preparing family meals frequently while still in high school. Many times there were unexpected guests, but at that age I didn't have sense enough to panic and my mother covered any shortcomings, so I developed a sort of "feeling" about people, food, and conversation. We had lots of company when I was growing up, and I was never afraid to ask if a friend (or two or three) could stay for dinner. Most of the time we ate our evening meal in the dining room, even if it was "just us four and no more!" Dinner time was usually a time when we lingered to recount the events of the day. This training helped me particularly in the early years of entertaining.

With the coming of children and more responsibilities I decided that I *had* to get organized. Making lists, no matter how sketchy, is one good step. You will have to decide how to organize yourself according to your personality, abilities, and type of entertaining. Try different ways and always be flexible.

Some general guides that almost everyone mentioned in some way are these.

1. Decide on kind of party, guest list, and date, and send invitations or telephone two weeks before the date (weddings, etc., one month before).

2. Write down your menu. Buy staple items a week ahead (spread out the cost!), buy the rest of the food no later than the day before the party. If possible cook and freeze several items ahead of time.

3. Collect items for centerpiece at least the day before.

4. Do heavy cleaning as early as possible. Check crystal, silver, china, linen to be sure everything is ready. Clean adequately but don't drive the family crazy scrubbing every nook and cranny. Be sure to sweep front walk, steps, and porch. "Pick up" yard (limbs, trash, etc.) if you don't have time to get the yard manicured.

5. Do all your errands the day before the party.

6. Decide what you're going to wear and be sure it is ready.

7. Set the table (for dinner or open house, lunch or morning —whatever) the night before.

8. Have entrance well lighted and check the windows across the front of the house. If you have shades or blinds, they should all be at the same level.

9. It's nice to have closet space to hang coats (include some covered hangers for fur stoles) and be sure you have someone (older son or daughter or close friend) designated to take coats for guests.

10. If you do not have a powder room, be sure that the bathroom to be used is accessible and that the guests do not have to wander through all the bedrooms.

11. There's nothing wrong with closed doors! Close the door to any room you do not want entered.

12. Party Day—do centerpiece, finish cooking, straighten house, clean guest bath (remove the "Do Not Use" sign before guests arrive!), check for dustcloth or other cleaning equipment left out, "twitch" pillows, relax and ENJOY!

Now, this suggestion may sound unnecessary but nevertheless let me remind you to turn on the front porch light (if it is an evening party) and the floodlights at least forty-five minutes before party time. My husband and I were invited to dinner at the home of a couple we hardly knew. We arrived a "safe" five or ten minutes late and had a real sinking feeling because there were no lights on in the front of the house and we wondered if we had the wrong house or the wrong date. After checking the invitation, the calendar, the time and address, we stumbled up the walk to the door. The hostess was in a state of undress, the children were zooming up and down the stairs, and the host had not arrived home. We were all completely unnerved and the evening was unfortunately unforgettable. If they had been close friends, we could have "pitched in" and made ourselves at home. Emergencies do happen to all of us, but even in the most difficult situations, every effort should be made to assure the guest that he is wanted and special.

Frances Moore has a great suggestion, and I plan to do it just as soon as I finish this manuscript! She says this: list all the people you want to entertain in the next few months. Break the list down into couples, single men, single women. Make a guest chart, using a loose-leaf notebook or card file. This will be a party diary: a permanent record of all the parties you give, including the dates, the people you invite, and the menu for each occasion. The more parties you give, the more notes you will have for future reference. (I can't wait to get started!)

When Guests Spend the Night

Overnight guests can be either lots of fun or lots of trouble. Here again the guest has a real responsibility to try to fit in with the household schedule. She/he shouldn't expect to sleep all day and visit all night. The guest should ask to be called in time for breakfast (this leaves it up to the hostess), be content to eat whatever is usually served, and not make any extra demands (especially early in the morning!). If the guest has to share a bathroom, he should inquire about school or work schedules and stay out of the bathroom for a lengthy shower till the troops are off.

Some more thoughts on guests:

1. I try to keep a "guest box" ready to pull out for overnight company. When I put fresh sheets on the bed and get out clean towels and washcloth, I just put these things on the dresser: a clean glass; fresh soap; hand mirror; a new toothbrush (someone always forgets), toothpaste, and mouthwash; and extra shaving equipment.

2. It is nice to be able to provide drawer or closet space and a place to open a suitcase.

3. You'll win an award if you provide a lamp for reading, a radio, and a clock (insomniacs like to keep up with the time!).

4. Make sure the shower/tub is clean and the children's rubber ducks are out of the way.

5. Add a personal "glad you're here" touch—a magazine or book, a small plant (such as African violet), and perhaps a carafe or vacuum bottle of hot chocolate, coffee, or tea, and a mug for the early riser. For that you'll win the five-star rating!

We really enjoy having our out-of-town friends spend the night in our home when they're in Atlanta for business or pleasure. We have so much more time together that way, and we just treat them like part of the family.

We also appreciate having international friends stay in our home. Being in homes helps them understand our country and culture better, and we enjoy that privilege when we are traveling abroad.

Let me hasten to assure you that we do try to be a little more dignified on those occasions, but it is hard when our sons forget and turn the stereo up full blast, both phones ring at the same time, and the dog is sulking. Our Swiss "adopted daughter" who spent a month with us several Christmases ago assured us that living in our household was like living in a national park. I wonder what she meant by that?

The kind of party you give, where you have it, and what you serve can be as wide as your imagination. It can be a farewell party, a welcome home party, a gathering of new acquaintances, a roundup of delayed passengers at an airport. Or it can be at your office, in your kitchen, your studio—wherever there's space for a group of people to gather, that's the place for a party. No matter how informal, it's a party when friends get together, break bread, and have fun.

The following chapters will give you some ideas that will help get you started.

The Great Outdoors

Spur-of-the-Moment Picnics

The first warm day of spring is a definite signal to start planning outdoor parties and picnics. First of all, there is something therapeutic about being in the open air. Almost any place will do—a park, backyard, patio, riverfront, field, top of a mountain—anywhere. And when you have a picnic, you don't have to worry about a centerpiece or other decorations—God has it all ready for you! Anne King and I packed a sandwich, an apple, and a jar of water each, hiked two miles up the Rabun Bald trail, and had our lunch out on a rocky ledge overlooking Sky Valley. It was soul restoring to both of us.

Sometimes it's fun to ask a family or two to bring a picnic basket to church and afterwards all of you go to a nearby park for Sunday lunch. The children can run off pent-up energy and the adults can relax. Clean up is only a garbage can away.

When our staff wives feel the need to get together and everything seems to be stopping us (some have jobs, preschool children, etc.), we decide to meet at a centrally located park, go dutch for delicatessen sandwiches, bring a diet drink, and have an uninterrupted fifty minutes or so to laugh or cry as the case may be. Anyway, we love this time together and should do it more often.

If you think men may not like a picnic, you should hear Roy Simmons tell about being in charge of a group of businessmen traveling in Scotland. They ordered picnic lunches packed and stopped by one of the rivers to eat. The heather was beautiful and the men had such a great time they didn't want to leave.

I don't think this fits in here, but I don't want to forget. When you go to Europe, be sure to rent a car and take to the back roads. Stop in a village at the "backerie" to get fresh-baked bread and sweets, add cheese from the cheese shop, and then get something to drink. Drive on and you'll find the perfect spot by a river on the side of an Alp to munch and soak up the soft soothing atmosphere. Of course, you don't have to go to Europe to experience this. Any family who has traveled in the United States in any direction surely knows the pleasure of picnicking at roadside parks and in our national forests.

For spur-of-the-moment picnics, you do not need to make arrangements with the parks department. If you are planning a huge family reunion picnic or something like that, most city and state parks have covered pavilions (in case of rain) and fireplaces for cooking that you should reserve.

If there are babies and creepers, please do think ahead for your own enjoyment. You'll probably want to take the playpen and stroller and provide protection from the sun. For toddlers and preschoolers plan to take baby-sitters along to provide constant supervision or be ready to swing, slide, and seesaw yourself. Older children are more easily kept entertained with ball games, frisbees, hide-and-seek and their own creative ideas. Our sons always enjoyed the plastic toy soldiers, cowboys, and Indians and spent hours setting up elaborate headquarters, battlegrounds and such while we picnicked by a shallow river-bank.

Eating out-of-doors is enjoyable any time the weather permits. A nice way to start the day is to have breakfast (at least juice and coffee) on the patio or in the backyard. This is usually a Saturday morning treat, but think how nice to get the children fed and off to school and have a nice, quiet, nerve-settling breakfast for you and your husband or just for you outdoors! And a good way to cut down on kitchen traffic is to serve those peanut-butter-and-jelly sandwiches and a drink for Saturday lunch on the backyard picnic table.

A well-planned picnic can be used for many occasions. The

picnic parties described here will spark your imagination for the next time it's your turn to entertain your group.

Picnic Basket Party

A picnic basket party is popular in many places in the South. Here are the steps in planning and two menus.

1. Collect or borrow straw breadbaskets or get small market baskets from a farmers' market or produce company.

2. Line the baskets with foil in case of spills. Then also line each basket with either a colorful cloth napkin or a novelty paper napkin, including a matching or complementing napkin for use.

3. Use card tables with plywood rounds (indoors or outdoors). For informal teen-age gatherings, the guests may sit on the floor.

4. Plan to use cloths on the tables to complement the napkins used in the baskets.

5. It takes longer than you think to pack baskets, so start early.

Menu One

Fried Chicken
Curried Fruit
Pimento Cheese Sandwich or Bun with Ham Salad
Skewer of Olives, Pickles, Cheese
One-half Deviled Egg
Ice Cream Cone Cake or Cookies
Lemonade

Isobel Donaldson

Mrs. Donaldson uses little brown wicker baskets with handles. She puts two small pieces of chicken wrapped in aluminum foil in each basket and puts the curried fruit in small containers covered with plastic wrap. The ice cream cone cake is made by baking cake inside cones and then icing with vanilla or chocolate to look like ice cream.

Menu Two

Fried Chicken
Pimento Cheese Sandwich or Barbecue on Bun
Cheese and Pickle Skewers
Tossed Salad   Mixed Fruit
Brownie or Butterscotch Bar
Iced Tea

Mrs. Clifford Campbell
Mrs. James R. Neill

You may want to use potato salad or bean salad and ham biscuits instead of chicken. There are any number of possibilities. (My personal note: if you are new at cooking, you might avoid total frustration by buying your chicken already fried from one of those carry-out places. Just hide the containers!)

For the cheese and pickle skewers alternate cheese cubes and pickles on a toothpick or party skewer. Use your favorite tossed salad, use dressing sparingly, toss as late as possible and pack in disposable clear cups covered with plastic wrap. For mixed fruit use cut-up apples, pears, melon, grapes, etc. Use ascorbic acid or dry lemonade mix to keep the fruit from turning brown. Package in clear plastic cups and cover with plastic wrap.

Tailgate Party

Betty and Earl Van Gerpen do a lot of entertaining by inviting friends and clients to events like horse shows, football games, or any spectator sport. This is really an excursion, and like all social get-togethers a picnic requires a lot of thought. Everyone loves a picnic, but for the one who has to prepare it, considerable planning has to be done. It is very difficult to assemble everything at the last minute, so plan ahead. Try to avoid messy foods, fragile foods, and foods that are apt to spoil. In packing, be sure to wrap each item individually, and if it is not easily recognizable, label it. Betty urges, along with other successful hostesses, making a list of items needed. Here are some of her suggestions.

1. Individual plates or baskets. Baskets lined with a cloth square are the easiest to handle, and once you have made the investment it is forever. Include attractive paper napkins.

2. Plastic knives, forks, and spoons that may be needed. (A picnic is really the *only* place for paper and plastic.)

3. Extra roll of paper towels; extra aluminum foil and plastic wrap.

4. Packaged disposable washcloths for hands after eating (or before).

5. Bottle openers.

6. Cooler with extra ice (lots of ice is particularly important on a hot day). Coolers are needed to keep food fresh.

7. Soft drinks.

8. If the day is cold, a huge vacuum bottle of coffee (don't forget cream or sugar).

9. Sharp knife (if any slicing is to be done).

10. Pickle picks (or toothpicks) for handling pickles and olives.

11. Plenty of cups for hot or cold beverage.

12. Large plastic bags for garbage.

13. Tablecloth.

14. Blankets, folding chairs, and folding table (if you have no tailgate!).

15. Individual packages of mayonnaise and mustard.

When assembling items for your tailgate party, think first of your guests. You want the atmosphere to be pleasant, so be enthusiastic from the beginning and always remember to be gracious. Let's face it. It *is* a drag to get things packed and into the car (a list and being organized helps), but this is a marvelous way to entertain a large number of friends before a sporting event when you must drive a distance. Friends who share your enthusiasm for the special event will be grateful to you for including them. If you include several carloads of friends, you should all plan to leave at approximately the same time so that you can park near each other if a large parking lot is to be used. A tailgate party is genuinely appreciated because it solves the stopping for lunch problem with its associated parking problem.

Be sure to allow ample time for the picnic because no matter how wonderful the food is or how attractively set up, if it's time for the kickoff, everyone will be impatient and your picnic will be spoiled. Arrive early and spread a casual tablecloth on the tailgate or folding table. A paper cloth will tear easily and is likely to be carried away by the wind. Anyway, paper cloths are expensive, and you can use the same casual cloth over and over.

Now for the menu! When planning, remember that you want food that is exciting, food that is easy to serve, *and* food that is good left over. It usually takes a while to get out of the parking lot after an event, so when guests get back to the car, it's nice to have some snacks to offer them. This is easily done when you have thought ahead and packed a little extra food. People are always hungry after a game, so instead of rushing to get in the line of cars and being impatient and frustrated trying to get out of the lot, just act in no hurry to leave. In your most gracious manner, set out the leftover food and enjoy your guests a little longer. They will love you for your thoughtfulness, and when the traffic has cleared, you can be on your way with everybody relaxed instead of being tense over the game and the traffic!

Suggested Menu

1. Stacks of sandwiches. *Thin* sliced ham, roast beef, turkey. Try rye bread for ham (buy rye bread with ground caraway seeds because some people object to the seeded bread), dark bread (pumpernickel or wheat) for the roast beef, and white bread for the turkey.

The sandwiches may be made the night before using only the bread and meat. *Omit* the mustard or mayonnaise as this will make the sandwich soggy. Have either individual mustard and mayonnaise or small containers of each that the individual can add to his own sandwich. Place the sandwiches in sandwich bags or wrap them securely in plastic wrap and store them in the refrigerator overnight. It is even better if they are placed in bags, then stacked and wrapped in damp towels. This is not absolutely necessary, but it makes them taste a little fresher the next day.

2. Fresh relishes. Clean and prepare celery, carrots, green onions, radishes, cauliflower, and cherry tomatoes. Place some of each in individual plastic bags and tie the top with a gingham or calico bow. Store in the refrigerator overnight. The bows take a little extra work, but your guests will love the extra effort.

Remember to prepare enough fresh relishes for after the game. Put extras in a large plastic bag.

3. Individual packages of potato chips. (The fifteen-cent size is best. The small ones for school lunches are too small). If someone is on a diet, he will not feel compelled to eat them, and you can take unopened packages home for school lunches.

4. Assorted cheeses. Adjust the size cheese to the number of people to be served. If it is a large group, buy two or three large rounds of your favorite cheeses. Take a cheese knife and cut as desired. Any left over can be used later at home. If the group is small, then the small rounds or wedges will do nicely.

5. Flat bread or crackers. Buy your favorite assortment. A flat gingersnap and a wedge of gourmandise cheese to have after the game are good.

6. Fresh fruits. Buy anything in season and lots of it (apples, plums, grapes, oranges, etc.). Wash thoroughly and store in plastic bags on ice in the cooler.

7. Dessert. Melting Moments (see recipes) wrapped individually.

When you pack the individual baskets, be aware of color. Coordinate the basket liners, the bows, and the napkins. It will look so pretty and your guests will appreciate your effort. It's just as easy to coordinate things; the secret is in the planning. After you have lined the baskets, put in a sandwich, potato chips, crisp relishes, and individually wrapped dessert. Always have extras of everything. Outdoor events make for healthy appetites.

After the game bring out the folding table or put the cloth on the tailgate and spread the fruit, cheese and crackers, and extra soft drinks. Your guests will be completely charmed (even the grumpiest loser) and in their eyes you will be the perfect hostess.

Tennis Party

Tennis has become one of the most popular sports among all groups both male and female. When there is a little sunshine in the sky, thoughts turn to tennis; public park courts and private club courts become crowded, and the sound of rackets swatting balls fills the air. To a tennis player nothing can be more exciting or relaxing than a social game of doubles. So why not plan a party around it?

Betty Van Gerpen finds this a good way to entertain friends and makes these suggestions. In making out your guest list give consideration to a congenial group—not only in personality but in playing skill. If most of the guests have been playing tennis for a while, it would be difficult for them to enjoy an afternoon of tennis with beginners mingled in. If you, the hostess, are just taking up the game, a few beginners would be appropriate. This is a fun time, not competitive; with a little careful planning, everyone will enjoy it.

Plan a round robin so that each guest will have a chance to play with every other guest. Keep score and have a prize for high score. The prize doesn't have to be anything more than a can of balls, but it stirs up excitement and adds to the fun.

If you don't have a court in your backyard, don't let that keep you from having a party! Perhaps your nearby park courts can be reserved, or if you belong to a tennis or country club, you may be allowed to use a court for your party.

Remember to have extra towels and balls. If it is a hot summer day or evening, you'll need to provide plenty of thirst quenchers. In addition to lots of ice water, mix chilled tonic water and fresh lemon juice. This is very refreshing. It is fun to eat by the court, so serving the food is easier in picnic style whether in the middle of the day or in the evening.

Make your guests feel special by providing individual baskets with handles or small galvanized pails. The pails are also a good investment in that you can use them over and over. A cloth square of gingham or any of your favorite fabric should be placed inside the basket or pail with a cloth napkin to match or coordinate with the liner. A nice touch is to have a personalized key chain attached to the handle as a memento of the occasion. These can be bought at any hobby shop and easily painted (they are wooden and come in various shapes).

Any of your favorite picnic menus can be used. Betty has

shared hers in the menu section. Guests may not be ready to eat at the same time, so it is nice to set up a table for the pails or baskets and the drinks. This is a very casual party and the atmosphere should be a very relaxing one.

Things to remember:

1. Invite congenial guests.

2. Have plenty of thirst quenchers and exciting food.

3. Provide chairs or blankets for guests to sit on.

4. Have extra towels and balls.

5. Keep scores on a large poster or blackboard.

So find a court and have a fun party that your tennis friends will long remember.

Golf Luncheon

A lot of entertainment takes place in homes surrounding golf courses. During the big tournaments many people invite their friends to drop in for a lunch break. It is a welcome respite to the fans and a great opportunity for spontaneous fun. Many times the hostess puts all the sandwich fixings out on the counter and lets each person make his own "Dagwood Special." Sometimes it is more elaborate with salads, but most people are starving from all that walking and are ready for a big sandwich, cake or cookies, and plenty of iced tea or lemonade. This is an ideal way to entertain business associates. If you want a centerpiece for a more elaborate pregolf luncheon, Frances Moore suggests cutting a piece of cardboard in the shape of a green. Cover it with green material; make the cup and put a flag in it. Make stick figures of a foursome and put them on the green with one figure putting. This can be a centerpiece one year and used again as an interest center on the coffee table or an end table.

Seasonal and Special Occasions

A Candlelight Dessert Party

Seasonal and holiday entertaining are naturals. There are more ideas for holiday entertaining than you'll ever have time to try. Cascile Knight has a candlelight dessert party for the deacons and their wives at Christmastime (about eighty people). This would be great for entertaining trustees or board members, any club, etc. Here is the way she does it. She has saved dozens and dozens of one-quart mayonnaise jars through the years to use for the party. She also saves candles year after year (those too short for other decorations are ideal for this). The candles are stabilized in the jars in slightly dampened builders' sand or in short plastic cups. These outline the drive and front walk as well as the shrubbery in both the front and back yards. The only light used inside the house is candlelight (even in the bathrooms!). The large table in the dining room offers a choice of several desserts including a beautiful pink strawberry cake that enhances the color of the centerpiece of pink roses. All these desserts are baked and frozen weeks ahead. (See the menu and recipe sections.)

Christmas Eve Dinner

The Kings have a traditional Christmas Eve dinner (after six o'clock communion) for the family. Anne uses an elegant centerpiece—usually a small tree made of tiny pinecones and sweet-gum-tree balls wired on a styrofoam cone and sprayed gold. Small red bows are also wired to the styrofoam and the tree is placed on a brass compote. On either side of the tree are placed brass candlesticks with red candles and hurricane shades.

Equally effective as a centerpiece for this occasion is fruit (lots of apples) on a brass, wooden, or crystal tray with brass candlesticks. You'll not want to miss this scrumptious menu, found in the chapter titled "Menus."

Place cards are nice to use, especially if there are teen-agers with dates. Anne gave the young people pixies made of green and red nylon net. The legs and arms were filled with peppermint candy. The styrofoam head had small hatpins forming the eyes and nose. Red felt was cut for the mouth, and red and green yarn was used at the hands and feet to tie the net. A pointed green felt cap was glued onto the head.

New Year's Eve Party

Whenever we can, Bill and I like to visit our very special friends, Anne and Bill King, who live south of Atlanta in Thomasville, Georgia. Anne and I grew up together in Ocala, Florida, went through high school and Stetson University, and are also Tri Delta sorority sisters. Bill King is a dentist, they are good Methodists, and when the four of us get together, our children begin to wonder about our sanity. We especially like to visit the Kings for their New Year's Eve party. There are usually five or six couples who come about half-past nine and stay to see the New Year in. The guests each bring their own steak (Bill King is the chef), and the hostess prepares a salad, baked apples, barbecue bread, coffee, and cake. As always it's the company as well as the food that makes the party.

New Year's Day Party

A New Year's Day dinner or whatever you would call it at four o'clock between games may be your answer to Football Fever. Norma Key finally went this route, and it has grown into a huge success—surpassing the Super Bowl. She decided to invite a few people for the traditional New Year's Day dinner of pork roast, black-eyed peas cooked in hog jowl (or ham hock), baked sweet potatoes, turnip greens, cornbread, and cherry cobbler.

The number grew too large for the kitchen so it was moved to the dining room with all the trimmings. One male guest said, "This is the first time I've ever been served black-eyed peas from a silver bowl!" It sounds good to me!

Birthday Party

If you have a big family, birthdays can keep you busy. For a family birthday dinner include special people the honoree would like to invite, grandparents, and family. Prepare a favorite dinner, bring out the good china, crystal, and silverware —the works. Put balloons on the mailbox even if it's Grandfather's birthday.

Fondue Party

One of my favorite dinner parties is a fondue party. This is especially good if you are having people who don't know each other. Everybody has to get involved in the meal, and there is so much conversation and laughter sparked by dipping in and out of the fondue pot that everyone feels comfortable. Fondue is versatile and good for patio or dining room. I can seat ten at our dining table and six at the table in the family room. We use a fondue pot on each end of the dining table and one on the round table. I use my regular china (fondue plates aren't necessary) and the sauces and relishes (for beef fondue) can be passed and put on the dinner plate. For this meal the table is crowded and there is a lot of movement, so keep the centerpiece to a trail of ivy and a few daisies or mums (or whatever you have) stuck in at the last minute to keep without water. No candles, please, there is enough heat from the cookers. Use washable place mats or tablecloth because this is messy but fun!

As our guests arrive, we like to invite them to the patio for tomato juice cocktail. (I use half Bloody Mary mix and half V-8 juice. It really packs a punch!) I don't usually serve finger food because it really isn't needed with a fondue dinner. While Bill and the guests take care of making the ice cream (I have the mixture ready ahead—chilled—so all they do is add ice and salt to churn), I finish up in the kitchen. Then while we eat, the ice cream is packed and "resting" till we are ready for it. Because the table after fondue looks so bad, we go to either the living room or the patio (if you have a suitable playroom, that would be nice) and serve the ice cream that the guests helped make, pound cake, and coffee. We wait at least forty-five minutes between dinner and dessert. It's more enjoyable that way. In the menu section you will find suggestions for beef fondue and cheese fondue dinners.

Our family considers it a special treat to have beef fondue "just for us." We learned to enjoy this in a cozy little restaurant that serves nothing but fondue in Berne, Switzerland. Our "adopted" Swiss daughter, Helene Ringgenberg, introduced us to the "real food" in her own home, in the "guest houses" in villages tucked away by lakes, and in "pensions" at the end of mountain trails. Fondue and hearty soups are a mainstay and so delicious. A tall glass of cold chocolate milk tastes better at a mountainside restaurant than anywhere else in the world!

That bit of travelogue is thrown in to remind you that wherever you go, you should bring home souvenirs of taste and smell; a special food that will bring back the memories of an evening when the violinists were strolling through the sidewalk cafe in Venice, of the "coffee ice" sipped in Florence, of those pungent cooking odors in the back country of Thailand. The senses of taste and smell trigger all sorts of memories in us. That's why all children should smell oatmeal cookies baking occasionally when they come home from school. It gives a nice warm glow all over.

Partying with Crepes

If an "Oscar" were given to the hostess who has devoted herself to unsurpassed excellence in entertaining, Betty·Van Gerpen would surely be the undisputed winner. Betty is an almost nonstop bundle of activity and ideas, and takes seriously the importance of entertaining not only just for the fun of it but also for her husband's professional responsibilities. The parties Betty describes are suitable for many occasions—church groups, political meetings, PTA board meetings, committee meetings, all women or both men and women. Betty is an encyclopedia of innovative ideas and choice recipes. The very nicest thing about her parties is that they are absolutely beautifully done (she does all the cooking); she is totally relaxed and obviously enjoys her own party. One of her favorite ways to entertain a large group is with a crepe party.

Now before you decide that crepes are way out of your culinary ability, just listen to this. Lisa, Betty's twelve-year-old daughter, makes crepes like a professional! It just takes some practice, and the more you experiment, the more you'll discover new ways to serve them. As Betty says, "Crepes are exciting and this type of party can be loads of fun." This portion on crepes is a paraphrase of all the things Betty has told me. Believe me, she knows about crepes. Just recently she served a crepe luncheon to two hundred ladies!

A crepe is a light delicate pancake and should be paper thin. Nothing is easier to prepare or more intriguing to serve than crepes. Everyone is fascinated and in awe, so if you serve crepes to your guests a few times, your reputation as a super cook and elegant hostess will be established forever.

Proper pans are important since the pan does most of the work. Choose a pan about five or six inches in diameter, and if it is Teflon coated, it will be easier to use. You will find many pans to choose from in the cookware section of a department store or in a cookware specialty shop.

When preparing crepes, pour in just enough batter to cover the surface of the pan. Cook on medium high heat and turn with a spatula when the edges begin to brown. Crepes have an inside and an outside. The side which cooks first is more attractive, so it should be used on the outside. *Remember*: crepes should always be very thin. As soon as each crepe is made, place it on a clean tea towel—right side up. If they are stacked this way while being prepared, they are ready to be stored in the refrigerator. They also may be filled immediately. For a party we strongly recommend doing them a few days ahead. A good hostess does as many things ahead as possible. Last minute details creep up, and it's very rewarding to have things prepared in advance.

This is a great way to serve a lot of people easily because with the crepes prepared in advance, all you need do the day of the party is fill and roll them. The filling should be carefully thought out. Almost as important as the filling is the garnish because the appearance of the dish is of *great* importance. Remember—nothing tastes good unless it looks good. Fillings and garnishes are discussed later in the recipe section.

Most crepes should be heated in a 400-degree oven for fifteen minutes. It is easier and prettier if they can be filled, rolled, placed in a buttered glass baking dish, heated, and then served in the same baking dish. (This helps keep the crepes warm also.) Have holders for the baking dishes. Betty uses silver, but you could use copper or brass depending on your style. It is wise to choose holders with a candle or wick underneath to keep the crepes warm for longer periods of time.

If you need several hundred crepes, then obviously you will not have enough baking dishes; so fill the crepes, store them on cookie sheets, and then transfer them to the dishes to be heated.

It is nice to have three or four kinds of crepes and always a large bowl of *fresh* fruit. Use china bread-and-butter plates, salad plates, and salad forks. Crepes are exciting so don't spoil your elegance with paper or plastic! Use luncheon-sized cloth napkins you have collected and made to coordinate with the other colors you will be using. Coordinate several colors to match the colors in your centerpiece. The little extra things will make your guests remember your party with fondness.

In planning your table, it is nice to have the beverage (coffee, tea, tea base punch) at one end, the *large* fruit bowl at the other, two kinds of crepes on either side and *fresh* flowers in the center. Since no one will be seated at the table, a rather tall centerpiece would be nice to use.

If your table is small, you may want to serve the beverage from another smaller table. Always think of your guests and what will make them most comfortable.

Someone will be needed in the kitchen at all times heating the crepes. You, the hostess, shouldn't do this. You should check from time to time but have everything arranged so that you can mingle with the guests and make them feel warm and welcome. You have created a nice setting for them—enjoy yourself, too.

You will also need someone very reliable to check the table so that near empty dishes can be removed and replaced with fresh ones.

Allow three large crepes or four small ones per person and have an ample supply. You may freeze leftover crepes (even if they have been filled) for short periods of time.

You will be busy cooking crepes for the brunch or luncheon so cheat a little and get the dessert from a bakery. One nice way to serve dessert is to have French cake or petits fours on small trays in the rooms used for the party. Miniature dessert pastries are nice because guests can pick them up and eat them with their fingers; therefore, you don't have to worry about dessert plates or extra forks. Served this way, guests will not have to return to the dining room for dessert.

Dessert crepes are best served after a regular seated dinner party. You want your guests to long remember the evening so make things unforgettable—soft music, good food, interesting guests, and crepes for dessert! You will find Betty's favorite crepe recipes in the recipe section.

Bridal Parties

Thomasville, Georgia, is renowned for its roses, but even more beautiful than the roses are the people who live there. To an outsider looking in, it seems to be an ideal place to live. Thomasville hostesses entertain with elegant teas, both private and in connection with the tour of homes during the famous fall festival. There are open houses during the holiday season, fish fries, and church group affairs. Dinner parties for from eight to twelve range from game dinners (quail, dove, and duck are popular in this area) to seafood dinners. Ice cream socials are favorites for any evening or Sunday afternoon. Three families usually go together for these and have from twenty-four to thirty people.

There are a lot of large parties given for brides-to-be in Thomasville, and several hostesses make it easy and fun. If you have never undertaken a really big party, you may appreciate a step-by-step example. Three friends in Thomasville combined forces to give a party honoring a bride-to-be last summer. It was planned and executed within two weeks. Here are the steps they took from start to finish.

> Bride's Coffee (for 200 to 225 guests)
> Three Hostesses: Mrs. Paul Hjort
> Mrs. Jack Kelly
> Mrs. Bill King (King home)

Gift to Bride: Williamsburg crystal
reproduction pitcher

1. Get invitation list and select date with honoree. Determine type of party.

2. Either write invitations or have them printed. If written, buy cards with floral borders; buy stamps.

3. Hostesses divide list. Can spend one morning together or actually divide list and take home.

4. Mail ten days before party.

Example Invitation One

Coffee

honoring

Miss Elizabeth Ausley

Saturday, the twenty-sixth of July

from ten thirty to twelve thirty o'clock

2720 Old Monticello Road

Anne King

Frances Hjort   Janis Kelly

Example Invitation Two

Mrs. Bill King

Mrs. Paul Hjort

Mrs. Jack Kelly

honoring

Miss Elizabeth Ausley

Saturday, the twenty-sixth of July

from ten thirty to twelve thirty o'clock

2720 Old Monticello Road

5. Buy small white cocktail napkins.
6. Buy small white lace doilies to secure cups.
7. Engage punch cups from a church, jewelry store, or rental agency.
8. Engage someone to wash dishes day of party.
9. Plan menu and divide cooking duties. The person in whose home the party is given does the beverage and just one food.
10. Plan servers and call one week (at least) prior to party.
11. Final total cost split equally.
12. All greenery in house two or three days ahead.
13. Friends need to help:
    a. Two to pour punch one hour each.
    b. One teen-ager or young adult to assist pourer.
    c. One adult to act as hostess in dining room for each hour.
    d. Three friends (true blue!) in kitchen to arrange food on trays and take to dining room.
    e. Children of hostesses (preteen and teen) keeping guest book (original, homemade) outside or in den depending on weather.
14. Coffee self-service in breakfast room from old brass tray, using brown quail china.
15. Silver punch bowl to be used in dining room. No cloth. Use silver serving trays.
16. Centerpiece: antique wedding bowl with roses and leather fern.

Menu

Cheese Biscuits
Petite Bran and Raisin Muffins
Cheese and Sausage Balls
Open Round Cucumber Sandwiches
Chopped Beef Sandwiches
Watermelon Balls   Cantaloupe Balls
White Grapes   Crescents
Tea   Punch   Coffee

Bridal Tea

To have a formal afternoon tea, only a few changes have to be made. The time should be from four to six o'clock and all hostesses should wear long dresses. Have printed invitations mailed ten days to one week prior to party. For a large home you need to ask friends to help with flow of traffic and to help with conversation. A suggested hostess gift for the bride is a small silver sandwich tray. A good menu would be Rolled Pickled Okra Sandwiches, Rolled Dill Pickle Sandwiches, Open-faced Cherry Tomato Sandwiches, Davis Sandwiches, Cheese Straws, Angel Kisses, Caramel Cake, Apple Cake.

Bridal Shower

A paper shower for a bride is a great idea. Invite no more than forty guests. Have it at night and invite guests to come at one time (for instance, eight o'clock). Serve coffee and favorite cakes. Gift items may range from cookbooks to toilet tissue—all needed in homemaking but not expensive to give. The centerpiece can be paper flowers. Paper plates and napkins may be used.

A plant shower is also good, with a plant centerpiece that is given to the bride.

Apartment Entertaining

My cousin, Wynelle MacMullen, is a five-foot-one-inch bundle of imagination and determination. She has adjusted well to apartment dwelling in a middle-sized town, and when she casually talks about having Arthur Godfrey as a dinner guest, you'd think she lived in a mansion. I asked her for some tips on entertaining in a small apartment, and she replied that it's essentially the same as if you lived in a house because it's your *home*.

If you are in the "early attic" phase of decorating, don't worry about it and for goodness' sake, don't apologize. *Your* mood reflects in your guests and they'll feel sorry for you and sorry they came. Those orange crates are the "in" thing now and "so versatile." It is best to buy furniture sparingly and be sure you know what you want so that your small quarters won't look junky or "busy." Too much furniture and things are distracting. Light, airy colors with special attention to good arrangement of furniture for conversation are helpful. In an apartment there is no basement in which to store things and not many closets in which to hide things just before a party, so you do have to plan ahead. (Don't forget to use under-the-bed space). I especially like the feeling of Wynelle's apartment because she has used shades of yellows and greens and has a lot of ferns and green plants to avoid that "shut in" feeling. She has convinced the maintenance crew that they must not trim the ivy that creeps out of bounds along her walkway. She cuts it herself and always has a supply for decorating. Your apartment can reflect your personality just as a house should.

The really hard part of entertaining is the very small kitchens in apartments or town houses with barely room for one person to turn around and very little counter space.

If you have a separate dining room, you are indeed fortunate; but if it's only a dining area off the living room, you probably should limit the guest list to the number you can seat at your table. A one-dish meal is a good idea for this because it eliminates too much clutter and a discouraged-looking kitchen. Try to serve the plates from the kitchen and plan menus that can be prepared ahead. Gauge your time and enjoy your party.

A buffet can mean just as much work as a seated dinner so plan ahead and choose your menu carefully. Plan a "do-ahead" meal so that kitchen counters may be used for serving. Utilize snack trays, end tables, coffee table, card tables, folding chairs, floor cushions, whatever you have or can borrow. Serve food that is easy to manage. It is awkward to balance a full plate and try to gracefully cut meat with a knife and fork. It is a good idea to use food that requires only a fork and possibly a spoon. Keep it simple.

Ocala, Florida, is noted for being "horse country," and a number of celebrities and VIPs are in and out of the area checking on their horses or orange groves and just relaxing in the country. Last summer some friends asked Wynelle to have a birthday party for Arthur Godfrey. This was a spur-of-the-moment party because they didn't know until that very morning that he was coming. Since he was flying his own plane in during the afternoon and was not expecting a party, the plans were kept simple. She arranged assorted cheeses and crackers on her largest cheese board and served a tall cold fruit punch while guests were seated around the coffee table. There was good conversation and laughter, and the honoree was given a tray filled with birthday packages including some gag gifts. Of course, there was a birthday cake along with the traditional song, and Mr. Godfrey made a wish and blew out the candles. He had a happy relaxed time with a few friends who cared about him. Celebrities need to feel the warmth of friendship. Don't be afraid of very important people because they are God's children, too!

You never know whom you might be entertaining on very short notice so keep a casserole in the freezer, the silver polished, and a good friend who doesn't panic and can do something besides wring her hands! Wynelle insists that you can do whatever you really want to do no matter how small your home may be.

Frances and John Moore have apartment entertaining down to a fine art. During the years they lived in New York City, Frances learned many plan-ahead tricks and a lot of ways to substitute when necessary. An overambitious hostess can wear herself out trying to produce a multicourse dinner in a two-room apartment. The attempted grandeur of the dinner can be nullified by the anxiety of the hostess that everything be right and by the constant clearing of the table for still another course. Just imagine the shambles of dishes in the kitchen afterward! It is much better to have a simple meal that you can handle easily and have everybody relaxed than to have a pretentious dinner that causes tension in both hostess and guests.

My husband and I went to a dinner party in the Moores' charming apartment recently. They have a partition between the living and dining area, but you enter the apartment through the dining area. There was absolutely no sign of table, china, or anything to suggest dinner. While we were having tomato juice in the living room and chatting with the other guests, Frances and John did a magic act very quietly. They opened the drop-leaf dining table, set it beautifully for eight, and had dinner on the table. I've never seen anything like it. Dinner was absolutely delicious, served without a hitch with both Frances and John making sure everything was right. They have obviously practiced till perfect! If you have a few problems at first, don't be discouraged and don't apologize. It will get easier each time.

Some important things to remember:

1. Avoid a cluttered look.

2. Keep the guest list to a comfortable number.

3. Plan a menu that can be prepared ahead of time and served easily.

4. Be aware of ways you can substitute, and be innovative.

Diplomats at Home and Abroad

First Families

The "first family" of any large institution lives in a state of continual entertainment. There are always faculty dinners and visiting dignitaries to be entertained. Lou Lolley's husband is the President of Southeastern Baptist Theological Seminary in Wake Forest, North Carolina. The newly renovated President's Home is a busy place. This is especially the case as the Lolleys' two teen-aged daughters add their activities to the milieu.

Lou's formula for being a successful hostess is this: honesty, simplicity, and unpretentiousness. A hostess may not know or choose to follow all the accepted rules of protocol, but her entertaining will be successful because of the spirit of hospitality that can be felt by everyone.

For a large sit-down dinner the Lolleys serve buffet style with extra tables set up in the living room and foyer. However, for a small group of from six to twelve, they prefer the host-and-hostess-served meal. For a large group Lou uses oven food that can do its own bubbling while she's doing other things. Occasionally she serves a "top of the stove" dinner of country ham and red-eye gravy, scrambled eggs, grits, and biscuits. This requires years of practice (and a few extra hands and feet would help)!

When foreign groups are to be entertained, it is nice to do something that is typical of your area. The Baptist World Alliance Executive Committee held its annual meeting at Southeastern Seminary last year, and Dr. and Mrs. Lolley entertained them at a *Pig Picking* (which originated in North Carolina).

For a pig picking, a whole pig is dressed, split, and cooked in a pit over charcoal for most of the day. (Some people cut oil drums in half and make grills for the pigs). It is called a pig picking because the guests file by and pick the meat off themselves. Lou's terse description, "Different," seems to fit perfectly!

Each guest was also given a gift bag of North Carolina products. This event was a great success. Along with the pig, the menu included cabbage slaw, potato salad, a green vegetable, and hush puppies. A whole pig will serve thirty to fifty people. They used two pigs for eighty people and had a lot left over. This was used later for barbecue.

Mrs. Henry Holley, whose husband is the Director of International Crusades for Dr. Billy Graham, travels the world with her husband. An interesting part of her life is time spent planning dinners, luncheons, and civic receptions in cities wherever crusades are held. This is done in the hotel where the affair is to be held, working closely with the manager of the food and beverage department of the hotel. In each city she selects foods that are popular or famous in that part of the world. Bettie's favorite dinner at home in Atlanta for international guests as well as local friends is:

Fresh Fruit Salad
Teriyaki Steak   Steamed Rice
Green Bean and Asparagus Casserole
Coconut Pie
Coffee

Look in the recipe section for directions on preparing these foods.

Foreign Service

The people who serve in the foreign service (representing *any* country) view parties with a great variety of feelings. A party is not just fun to the diplomatic community, it is part of a job. To some degree the oil that keeps the wheels of the world turning is applied at these occasions. Recently, while we were representing President Ford at the inaugural ceremonies for Dr. William R. Tolbert as President of Liberia, West Africa, we were very aware of the part that entertaining plays in holding the world together. When a party is given and invitations are issued to members of the diplomatic corps, there is no question but that they appear and adhere to accepted protocol. Each nation has its own way of doing things, and a good briefing is essential before anyone steps into a new situation. Opinions, information, and impressions are given and received during these social occasions. It is fascinating to be at a dinner that is literally a world affair. The representatives of each nation are there (with their spouses) to see and hear and to be seen and heard. If you can have a pleasant social occasion with official representatives, it is easier to negotiate details of an agreement.

Our host and hostess for our visit to Liberia were Chargé d'Affaires Maurice Bean and his charming wife Doty. We are between ambassadors in Liberia and so Maurice has been appointed "acting ambassador" for the interim. The diplomat's wife plays a vital role in the success or failure of her husband's career. Of course, I think this is true in any profession whether it's foreign service, pastor, missionary, or corporation president. It almost has to be a team effort to be effective. For five days and nights the Beans and other personnel in the United States embassy were kept busy seeing that we were comfortable, entertained, and fed, and that we got to official functions on time and in proper order. This was not just an isolated five-day stint. After we left, Doty wrote that "from the inaugural activities, we went directly into a medical conference with the usual ceremonies, receptions, dinners, teas (for wives of delegates), luncheons, and abstract parties. During this time there was the wedding reception for President Tolbert's son and his bride, the wedding of the vice president's daughter, and a state visit by Princess Ashrof from Iran." Foreign diplomatic service sounds so glamorous, but it's hard to keep such a rigorous schedule and look and act glamorous on three or four hours sleep a night.

To capture Doty Bean in words is as difficult as trying to

package a Fourth of July fireworks spectacular. She is an animated, friendly human being who exudes warmth and fun. Because entertainment is part of the job for the Beans, I asked Doty to give some input to this book. In the midst of all that was going on, she did; it's good, honest facts and fun and, believe me, problems occur in the best-planned parties.

I am going to paraphrase Doty's contribution. In Monrovia, Liberia, the morning Pan Am flight brings the visiting dignitary or group who must be met and briefed by the embassy staff before early afternoon appointments with the local government officials. This calls for a working lunch, and two things can be counted on. The flight will be late and the visitor is almost always suffering from jet lag or Montezuma's revenge (stomach upset). Doty says she makes lunch fast before he falls asleep and makes it light because he'll most likely lose it immediately!

It is not unusual for Maurice to call at ten o'clock in the morning to ask, "How would you like several guests for luncheon *today?*" It is likely that the guests are seated in his office and since they are probably old friends, Doty controls the desire to scream into the phone. It is easier to be an enthusiastic hostess when there's a casserole on hand. Doty always keeps two or three sizes of casseroles to pull out of the freezer. One of her favorites is leftover chicken with mushrooms, wine, cream of chicken soup, and noodles. It looks good and crusty. All that is needed is a salad and good bread.

The Beans feel that everyone is happier in an informal setting. Service for dinner (or luncheon) for more than eight is always served buffet. Thirty guests can be seated comfortably in the dining room by using twelve at the dining table and three round tables of six. Another round table is used for serving. If the group is evenly divided by sex, the ladies are asked to choose a dinner partner and proceed to the buffet. If the group is uneven (often in developing countries, wives don't attend even though they are invited), the ladies go first and are requested not to bunch up at one table. Some hostesses are quite adamant about spouses sitting at the same table or next to each other. But often there are language difficulties, and one spouse may feel uncomfortable if not close enough to ask questions of the other to follow the conversation. The round tables and free choice of dinner partners made by the ladies keep anyone from becoming annoyed because of his or her rank and who sits next to whom or at which end of the table. (Foreign service types can really be paranoid about protocol, precedences, etc.)

The Beans have only served in the tropics and can usually count on flowers from their garden except when the insects have invaded. They use lots of greenery and few blossoms. On the coast they find beautiful shells and driftwood to use for decorating purposes. Doty has potted feather Boston fern in seashells to use on small tables. For color a hibiscus or several frangipani blossoms can be added. In West Africa the bright Fonti prints and lovely tie-dyes are popular table coverings with matching napkins.

Most foreign service families work together at party time since there is so much entertaining to do. The children become accustomed to meeting people from all walks of life. At receptions the youngsters often help pass platters, park cars, direct guests to buffet tables, and so forth. This is easier with some children when they are quite young and eager to be included in grown-up activities. Then the teen-age "Do I *have* to?" sets in, and you can only hope for the best. (No matter where you are in the whole world, the teen-ager is the same.) The Beans include their teen-aged daughter J.J. on the guest list and tell her the option is hers. She usually appears late, to "make an entrance," and enjoys being with the people.

Homes and families are basically the same everywhere. Even pets get into the act. The Beans have a German Shepherd who has caused some traumatic moments both before and during parties. One time she consumed eight beautiful steaks that were thawing for dinner! You can imagine the anguish and changing of plans!

If you think that foreign service wives don't have to know how to cook, you are very mistaken. Doty told me of an occasion that would strike panic in the heart of any hostess. When Maurice was the American Consul in Ibadan, Nigeria, they had planned a reception for about one hundred people. They had a good cook, so after making the plans, Doty wasn't worried about anything except what she would wear. After dressing, she went to the kitchen for that last-minute check and found almost nothing finished. No trays were done. Nothing was done! The pastry shells were empty, the hard-cooked egg whites were just sitting there empty, and there was no sauce for the shrimp. The cook was in a daze and seemed not to know what to do next. Doty tried to get him started so she could get to the guests, but the extra help they always counted on didn't arrive and she spent the whole evening in the hot kitchen. The two regular stewards were very good, but there is just so much that two people can do. Fortunately, three other consulate wives were on hand and did a great job passing hors d'oeuvres. Finally, Doty sneaked upstairs, changed clothes, and freshened her makeup in time to tell the guests good-night. The funny thing was that no one realized she hadn't been present. The group was so large that everyone thought she was somewhere else. Doty realized an unexpected triumph from the traumatic evening when guests commented that the food "which is always so good at your parties was even better tonight."

Three things Doty suggests for successful entertaining:

1. Keep smiling no matter what goes wrong.

2. Be prepared because there is virtually no time a diplomatic (or corporate) wife is exempt from entertaining.

3. Don't sweat the small stuff.

You will find one of Doty's favorite desserts (Coquilles Venus) and an idea for easy hors d'oeuvres in the recipe section.

I'm glad I don't have to feel responsible for keeping the wheels of world affairs oiled!

Mr. and Mrs. Walter H. Bunzl are the official representatives of the Austrian government here in Atlanta. Mrs. Bunzl's official capacity is the Chancellor of the Austrian Consulate. This office is one that sounds glamorous but actually involves a lot of time and work. When any citizen of Austria is in need of help in the Atlanta area, the Bunzls are called to work things out, referring any major crisis to the ambassador in Washington. Many responsibilities other than entertaining visiting dignitaries are involved. As I listened to her relate some of the problems they have to try to solve, I decided that the title "Chancellor" is a fancy cover-up word for counselor and hard work!

Mrs. Bunzl strongly advises that when entertaining, the host and hostess share equally the responsibility for making each guest feel that he is the guest of honor.

A good suggestion offered by Mrs. Bunzl for a seated dinner is to have two tea carts, one at each end (host and hostess) with the same food on each so that he serves half the guests and she serves half. She says it is also helpful to have everything (meat, vegetables) on two serving platters rather than many smaller containers. And she always has a bowl of whipped cream handy for coffee and almost anything else! There is always at least one Viennese Sachertorte in the freezer "just in case."

Mrs. Bunzl's favorite menu is duck served with cherries and orange slices, wild rice, string beans, salad (white asparagus marinated two hours in oil and vinegar), and coffee served after dinner with a whipped-cream dollop. For demitasse, Swiss mocha (available in the supermarket) with a trace of coffee liqueur and whipped cream. For a delicious dessert she suggests strawberries marinated in wine for twenty-four hours and then served with whipped cream in sherbert dishes.

Consul General and Mrs. Stephen S. F. Chen of the Republic of China are a delightful couple to know. I asked Mrs. Chen to suggest some Chinese recipes and she graciously provided a menu and the recipes. Rosa Chen says that a typical Chinese dinner usually consists of ten to twelve courses served one by one on a round table for twelve. Since it is difficult to do this without a cook, she recommends a six-course buffet dinner. You see, everyone has to be flexible, so don't be afraid to improvise when you need to do so.

Buffet Dinner for Eight to Ten People

Oil-dripped Chicken
Shrimp with Cashew Nuts
Sweet and Sour Pork
Fried Rice   Egg Rolls
Almond Jelly

Dr. Rosaio An and her husband, Dr. Nack Young An, are a charming Korean couple who make their home in Atlanta. Both of them are political science teachers. Dr. Nack Young is a professor at Georgia State University and Dr. Rosaio An teaches at Atlanta University. We were in their home not long ago to meet the Korean Ambassador to the United Nations. It was a delightful evening and reminded us of the pleasant parties we had been a part of when we visited Korea last year. One of our favorite Korean dishes is bulgogi (Korean barbecued beef). I asked Mrs. An to give us a sample menu for a Korean dinner party and was delighted to find bulgogi on the menu.

Menu For A Korean Dinner Party

Bulgogi   Mandu (Korean wanton)
Red Snapper with Mushrooms
Japchae (assorted vegetable dish)
Rice   Cucumber Salad
Fruit Bowl
Oriental Tea

One of the nicest things that ever happened to our church and to our family in particular has been the delightful family whom we helped settle in Atlanta when they had to leave family and all their worldly possessions in Cuba. Mr. and Mrs. Rafael Reyes, daughter Damaris, and son David are now happy citizens of the United States and we are proud to claim them. They have a beautiful garden every summer and they share the vegatables with us. Dinner in their home is scrumptious! Directions for making the foods in this menu are in the recipe section.

A Cuban Menu

Avocado Salad   Bread
Roast Pork
White Rice   Black Beans
Fried Green Plantains
Milk Pudding Cake
Coffee   Iced Tea

Especially for You, the Minister's Wife

At the alumni luncheon of Southeastern Baptist Theological Seminary my husband and I were seated with a group of younger ministers and their wives. The talk among the women drifted to entertaining and finally one said in desperation, "Well, I've decided I'm not having any more parties. No matter what I do, I get criticized. I can't even have any friends in for coffee without some of the people complaining loudly that I'm a snob. I'm just going to stay home and dry up." Then they all turned to me and said, "What do *you* do about entertaining?"

Now I must say that for a young minister's wife in a small- to middle-sized town entertaining can create a hornet's nest. I think there is a big difference in what can be done in a small town and small church and in a city and a big church. Let's face it, everybody in a small town knows the comings and goings of everybody else and especially the preacher's family. It takes years to learn how you personally can deal with your situation. Don't allow yourself or your family to be dominated or manipulated by any one family or group of families. You especially have to be aware of this when you first move into a new community. Do not ever allow anyone to corner you and demand to know *why* you can't come to their party. The minister's family could spend nearly every evening being guests in someone's home. You should limit your social engagements and preserve certain evenings for your own family at home. You can always say with a smile in your voice, "Thank you, we always enjoy

being with you, but we have plans for the evening." *Never* feel
that you have to give any other explanation even if there is one.
You *do* have plans to be at home. Try to avoid being with the
same group of people frequently (even if you enjoy them). This
establishes a clique and is devastating.

One rule we have had for twenty-two years is that we never
accept a social engagement for Saturday night. There is no way
you can be pulled apart by people Saturday night, and then get
yourself and your children put together and be worth anything
on Sunday all day. The Church School classes will soon learn
this if you are unwavering, and people will respect you for it.
When they really want you, they will consult your calendar
first. However, some group (or person) will try every week to test
your rule. *Be firm!* After all, what is most important—being the
jovial party favorite on Saturday, or standing before the whole
church Sunday morning with an unprepared heart? The sermon
should be ready by midweek, but the heart has to be in tune with
our heavenly Father. It will make the difference in your
husband's ministry.

Lealice Dehoney and Cascile Knight both agree that the
minister's family, perhaps more than any other, needs a time
when they can be themselves and really enjoy good friends. You
don't have to talk about it or mention the names of those you've
had in your home. Just assume that you have as much right as
anyone else to have friends.

While we were in small towns and churches, we found that we
were happier and could be more relaxed with couples outside the
church. I was in a garden club and my college sorority alumni
group, and this, along with Bill's Chamber of Commerce and
Kiwanis activities, gave us a wide range of community friends
and broadened our interests and influence.

Perhaps it's not so much whom you entertain in your home as
giving the appearance in public that you have only a few
friends. Avoid always sitting with the same group in church or
at any church dinner. Sit in a different place every Sunday. If
you really mix and mingle and are open and friendly when
you're with the church as a whole, the critics will subside.

In many churches there are some who feel that in order to

have a prestigious party they have to have the minister and his wife there. And you do have to guard against this form of manipulation. Lealice suggests that it is good to include new people in after-church fellowships. She likes to have a few people over after church and include new members so that they will feel more comfortable in their new church situation.

We started in a church with around two hundred members and now at Wieuca Road we have about forty-five hundred, so you can see that the same things that worked with two hundred are impossible now.

Let's start with the two hundred. To begin with, the house was totally inadequate for a pastor's family. The only dining area was in the kitchen, and the living room was a huge nine by twelve. So my entertaining was limited to Sunday School classes and a once-a-year dessert party for the deacons and their wives. Part of our ministry in that church was to teach them that the minister's life-style is not the same as theirs. A large healing ministry takes place in the warmth and fellowship of church groups in the pastor's home. I entertained in cramped quarters as a teaching tool.

Our next church was middle-sized with a nice adequate parsonage. In addition to our personal entertaining, I started something that I still do. I ask each ladies' Sunday School class (or co-ed class) to schedule one of their meetings at our home during the church year. I provide a very simple dessert (usually cake) and coffee or punch or apple juice, depending on the size of the class. It is important to keep everything very simple and just be very comfortable. Cake and coffee and a pitcher of ice water are all that is necessary! In our middle-sized church the Woman's Missionary Union needed a boost, so I had each of the circles once a year.

Now for the mind blower! We had a Christmas Open House each year for the whole church congregation! We never knew how many would come. My mother and I baked and froze Christmas cookies (Spritz) beginning in October each year. We made ahead and froze Pickups and Cheese Straws. There's no problem for decorations at Christmas except keeping toddlers and puppies and kittens out of the Christmas tree! For weeks

ahead Bill worried that everybody would come (what would we
do if we ran out of food?), then as the date drew closer, he began
to worry that nobody would come. (When he worries, there's no
need for me to bother!) It always worked out beautifully! We had
a lot of retired people who needed extra attention at the holiday
season, and they appreciated this so much. The other members
came also and it always seemed to flow very nicely. One thing
that has been true at all our parties: the men always congregate
in the kitchen, prop themselves against the sink and refrigerator, then ask, "Am I in your way?" For some unexplainable
reason I consider this a compliment, I think?

The first few years in Atlanta we did the Christmas Open
House following the same preparation procedure on a larger
scale. (Don't *ever* call anything you do an "annual" affair. You
don't want to have to move to get rid of it!) Then the church got
so big that it was just impossible to issue an open invitation not
knowing how to plan. Now we go to as many Christmas parties
given by Sunday School departments as we can (if they aren't on
Saturday night!) and try to see a lot of people in that way in a
social setting.

The last party I had that was an open invitation to the church
ladies was a welcome party for the wives of two new staff
members. When the invitation first appeared in the church
newsletter stating that all the ladies of the church were invited,
I had a number of calls inquiring about my mental health. Betty
Wilbanks, wife of our associate pastor, said, "Well, I have doubts
about your sanity, but what can I do to help?"

I had so many offers to help "crazy Carolyn" and we kept it so
simple that it was a breeze. I decided that twelve cakes (such as
pound cake—anything that didn't require a fork) could be cut in
small servings as we needed it; Polly Pledger made Cheese
Straws; we served punch in the family room and coffee in the
dining room, and the response was great. Friends made most of
the cakes and helped keep the trays filled, and it was a lot of fun.
Many women came who were new members, and everyone
seemed to appreciate the effort.

I must tell you that our staff wives are an integral part of our
church entertaining. They each assume the hostess role,

and I could never attempt these wild schemes without their help. It is important, if possible, for the ministers' wives to keep moving from group to group and make sure they are seen and speak to everybody. Don't ask them to serve in the kitchen. Hire someone or ask a *very* special friend to do that. Use every church function as an opportunity to improve public relations for everybody!

When we moved to Atlanta over a decade ago, it was still the era of the lavish, catered afternoon teas, and I almost withdrew into my shell because (1) that wasn't my style, (2) I couldn't afford it, (3) I didn't like it, (4) I was scared to death. I should have put number four first in order! We moved here in August and by December I had talked myself into having an Open House for all the congregation. Mother and I baked and froze while Bill paced the floor, wringing his hands. Mrs. Bonner Spearman helped decorate, deacons and their wives took turns helping to greet and serve, the staff stood by and did all the little things we forgot about, and Bill had a marvelous time and decided he had had a great idea!

I recommend an Open House party if you have the physical and emotional stamina and if your church is in the mid-size range. Learn to make Quick Mix Spritz press cookies and freeze them. At the party serve the cookies, a couple of plain pound cakes cut in rectangular pieces, thin sliced fruitcake (bought or homemade), cheese balls and crackers, and some nuts. Use a punch recipe that can be mixed in the punch bowl by opening cans of juice and pouring into the bowl. Borrow a huge coffee maker from the church. Use white paper cocktail napkins for a large crowd. Buy extra juice and ginger ale in case you need it; it will keep for later use. The important thing to remember is this: people realize that you don't know how many to prepare for so they usually take small servings. If you do run low, say, "Well, I am so flattered that so many people came. I'm sorry we are low on food, but we can still enjoy talking." Just don't fall apart; remain gracious and *calm.* How you handle the situation will be all over town in no time flat, and you'll give encouragement to the faintest heart. Let's face it, as the minister's wife or the wife of a church staff member, you are on display. What you do reflects on the church, and you can be a great influence in the community. I have heard too many snippy remarks about some preacher's wife who "thinks she's better than anybody else and demands extra attention or service." Well, I always consider the source, but there is just enough truth in that to hurt us all. I have several ideas that I'll put in here, and you may disagree violently. All I can say is that they work for me and from my observation the happiest ministers' wives have this basic philosophy.

1. People appreciate attention, especially from you—so give it graciously. The more you give, the more you *feel* like giving.

2. Don't carry a chip on your shoulder—it only burdens you.

3. Take every opportunity to mix and mingle and show interest and warmth to *all* age groups.

4. Bill and I use Wednesday night church suppers, WMU luncheons, and other such occasions to wander from table to table pouring coffee or tea and talking. This gives us all a nice warm feeling. Head tables where the pastor and wife sit and are served are obsolete and not good public relations.

5. If you become a people person and express warmth generously, you will have more love coming back to you than you can absorb. Even if you are shy (I am basically an inward person), you can develop your own style of friendliness, and it becomes easier through the years.

These basic attitudes apply no matter what your husband's profession is. It's simply a matter of warmth and concern. Anything that smacks of being manipulative is unfair and deserves all the criticism that it will incur.

If your husband were a physician or attorney, you would do the necessary niceties to help, not undermine, his success. The same rule applies to the minister's wife. You are not the associate pastor and should not be expected to be able "to be all things to all people." Just develop your own style, a sweet, flexible disposition, and be yourself. They'll love you for it. I think that you can entertain personal friends as often as you like as long as you balance it nicely with entertainment that includes a wide section of the church over a period of time.

To be specific let me list some examples. You will have lots of your own, I'm sure.

1. A group of the Woman's Missionary Society has helped Cascile Knight over a number of years in having a buffet luncheon for new church members and new people in the city. The ladies each help prepare the food and Cascile gets the house and tables ready. While waiting for everyone to arrive, the guests enjoy the camellia garden off the patio.

2. Dr. and Mrs. Knight also entertain the students home from college at Christmas after their Student Night program.

3. Dr. and Mrs. Wayne Dehoney enjoy entertaining leadership groups, deacons and wives, and others with making homemade ice cream in the yard. Many times when you do this, people will call and say, "Can I bring a freezer?" or "I'll bake a cake." Take all the help you can get. If no one offers, then it's up to you to provide. If it's an extremely large group, you can call some of your friends and cry, "Help!" Another variation on the ice cream party is to have a banana split party. It's easier than homemade ice cream but more expensive. Buy commercial ice cream in five-gallon cartons in three flavors, pounds and pounds of bananas, and lots of different toppings and nuts. Lealice has collected some banana split dishes, but you can also get them from ice cream parlors or places like the Dairy Queen—they are plastic and can be washed and used again.

4. Have a party for the new deacons and their wives (rotating system) the Sunday evening after they have been ordained or installed. It is nice to have all the deacons, but in a large church it becomes a problem. (We have sixty-nine deacons and eight staff ministers so that would be about one hundred and fifty-four people!)

5. Other groups you can invite into your home are leadership of the Church School and Church Training; the women's missionary leadership; enlistment coffees; the planning committees for various groups. Committees that work so long and hard need to be appreciated. Potluck suppers for some of these would be good—you furnish the meat, bread, and drink. You can do a lot of this in a small church. This type of fellowship makes a better working relationship for the pastor and the leadership.

6. Frequently it is helpful to have several parties in one week. If you have a clean house and your serving "stuff" out, why not just double everything (if you can) and do it again!

7. Have age groups of teen-agers in your home after church. It is important for them to see you as real people.

8. If you don't have a department or class for singles, you should. Be sure they are included in your entertaining schedule.

9. The Dehoneys have a reception for visitors after the eleven o'clock worship service. It is a great idea especially for downtown churches or churches in rapidly growing areas. Keep it simple—juice and coffee, or cokes and coffee. The main point of this is for fellowship. At Walnut Street Church they use the activities building for this function, and Lealice recruits deacons and wives (with no small children) to help with the "hostessing." They use this as a time to tour the building and learn about the recreation program of the church. As Lealice says, "It's just sort of another way of selling your church. It takes about forty-five minutes depending on how many visitors we have. It makes your lunch late, but it is very worthwhile, and we've had such a good response."

We decided to try this at Wieuca. We are fortunate to have a lovely room just under the sanctuary, so it is very easy for visitors to find their way. When we first started, Betty Wilbanks and I were totally responsible for getting people to help, set it up, etc. However, now we have four couples(who have no Sunday family responsibilities) who rotate the responsibility each Sunday of the month. They get their own helpers, set it up, and clean and lock up at the end. They are behind-the-scene heroes, and we really couldn't do without them. They are careful to choose helpers who are friendly and outgoing; our staff families stop by for a few minutes; Bill comes in as soon as he gets free at the door; and Betty and Oliver Wilbanks (associate pastor) and I are always there at the door to welcome them after they have signed the guest book.

This is a great idea for any church in an area of resort or commercial growth. You might want to do this seasonally if your community is relatively stable.

10. Dr. and Mrs. Knight have a delightful candlelight dessert party at Christmas. The details of this are in the chapter entitled "Seasonal and Special Occasions."

Random Notes

Several people have asked my husband and me whether or not we are embarassed when offered alcoholic drinks. This is only a problem if you let it be. At all the diplomatic receptions we've been to in every country there are always two waiters side by side—one with champagne or whatever and one with ginger ale, orange juice, or tonic water. You'd be surprised how many people opt for the nonalcoholic beverages. I especially like tonic water with a twist of lemon or lime (it isn't sweet like ginger ale). Often people will follow our example—in Korea many times the guests all take whatever the honorees have. Just be yourself and don't make any big deal or make anyone uncomfortable about it. You know, some people don't "come alive" till they've had an alcoholic drink, so for goodness' sake, be happy and pleasant and you'll be a good advertisement. As for being afraid someone won't enjoy coming to your party because you don't serve alcohol, don't give it a second thought. If you have good food, interesting conversation, and pay attention to your guests, they'll have a good time. Only an alcoholic would be totally miserable.

Don't cut yourself off from certain functions because you're afraid alcoholic beverages will be served. There are human beings who need your loving touch in all realms of society. If you stay away, you'll never know what your presence could have meant to someone or how you could have changed the tone of an entire gathering.

Develop a happy, pleasant disposition and you'll be on the most-wanted guest list!

Conclusion

Whether you live in a small Southern town or in a New York City apartment; whether you are in the foreign service in Monrovia, Liberia, or a pastor's wife in North Carolina, the secret to having a successful party is within you, the hostess. Relax; have the kind of party that suits you; be honest and unpretentious; let the warmth of your personality come through; let each guest know you care about him/her personally.

There are many ways of reaching out to people. A party may seem to be a rather frivolous way to do so. However, there are people who will respond to an invitation to a party but reject other overtures of friendship. Both the hostess and guests have a unique opportunity to respond to the needs of others in a relaxed, pleasant atmosphere. Our influence should not be restricted to just one little segment of life. The way we respond to people wherever we are should be our gift of love reaching out.

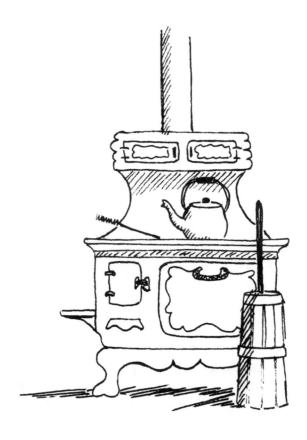

Menus

Lunch for Four on a Hot Summer Day

Tomato stuffed with Chicken Salad
on bed of crisp lettuce
Marinated Green Beans
Congealed Lime Gelatin Salad
Crackers   Potato Chips
Orange Chiffon Cake
Iced Tea

Frances Moore

Lunch for Four on a Cold Winter Day

Chili
Rye Bread
Tossed Green Salad
Grape-Nuts Pudding
Coffee

Frances Moore

Ella Moore's Dainty but Hearty Luncheon

Chicken Salad
Tomatoes/Asparagus
Cucumber Slices
Pimento Cheese Finger Sandwiches
on bed of crisp fresh salad greens
Sherbet or Ice Cream
Coffee

Tennis Party

**Fried Boneless Breast of Chicken
on Seeded Bun
Picnic Style Creamed Potatoes
Asparagus Vinaigrette with
Water Chestnuts
Fresh Fruit with Chocolate Meringues
Chilled Tonic Water and Fresh Lemon Juice**

Betty Van Gerpen

Tailgate Party

**Ham, Turkey, Roast Beef Sandwiches
Carrot Sticks, Celery, Green Onions, Radishes
Cauliflower, Cherry Tomatoes
Individual Packages of Potato Chips
Assorted Cheeses
Fresh Fruit
Melting Moments
Soft Drinks   Coffee**

Betty Van Gerpen

Young People's Saturday Lunch

**Bar-B-Burgers   Baked Beans
Potato Salad with Chips and Pickles
Brownies   Cokes**

Frances Moore

Golfer's Delight

**Chicken Curry with Condiments over Rice
Congealed Black Cherry Salad
Baked Devil's Float
Rolls   Coffee**

Frances Moore

Beef Fondue Dinner

**Cubed Beef
Rice and Water Chestnuts**

Apples and Carrots Casserole
Broccoli Puff
Various steak sauces placed in
small serving containers
Pepper Relish
Homemade Ice Cream with Pound Cake
Coffee

Carolyn Self

Cheese Fondue Dinner

"Self-Style" Neufchâtel Fondue
French bread cubes, olives, pickles, cherry tomatoes,
tiny sausages, cooked sliced carrots to dip
Marinated Shish Kabob   Rice
Homemade Rolls or Biscuits with Butter
Water   Iced Tea
Homemade Ice Cream
Coffee

Carolyn Self

"Dinner for Six"

Strawberry Soup
London Broil   Baked Potato
Broccoli
Rolls   Relish
Baked Custard   Coffee

Frances Moore

Make Ahead
Chicken Tetrazzini Dinner

Tomato Juice
Chicken Tetrazzini
Peach Pickle Salad
Relish tray of carrot, celery, pickles, etc.
Lemon Chiffon Pie
Tea   Coffee

Mrs. Tom Vann, Jr.

Menu Suitable for Fixing Ahead

Chicken and Wild Rice Casserole
Green Salad   Rolls
Million Dollar Pie
Coffee

Wynelle MacMullen

Dinner Menu

Chicken Breast Supreme
Wild Rice
Broccoli, Asparagus Casserole, or
Green Beans with Almonds
Pecan Pie or Fresh Fruit Cup with Cointreau
Coffee

Nanci Simmons

Nanci and Roy Simmons' Favorite Dinner Menu

Flank Stead   London Broil
Potato Casserole
Broccoli or Asparagus with Hollandaise Sauce
Fresh Mixed Fruit (in season)   Rolls
Pecan Pie
Coffee   Tea

Buffet for Large Group

Thin-sliced Ham in Tiny Biscuits *or* Party Rolls
Crab Bake
French Green Beans with lemon pepper and melted butter
Fresh Fruit Bowl
Cheese Tray
Selection of Pickups, Pound Cake, etc.
Water   Coffee

Carolyn Self

Easy Buffet

Party Punch
Crackers   Cheese Spreads
Sliced Baked Ham   Sliced Roast Turkey

American Cheese and Swiss Cheese
Rye, Whole Wheat, and White Breads
Mustard   Mayonnaise
Olives, pickles, radishes, celery, lettuce
Pound Cake
Coffee

Wynelle MacMullen

Ella Moore's Coffee
(25 to 35 people)

Large Coffee Cake
in pan to be sliced at the table
2 or 3 large fruit-filled, glazed Coffee Cakes
(frozen—heated and cut into 1-inch strips)
5 dozen Sausage Balls
2 pounds thinly sliced Baked Ham and/or Turkey
Brown Party Bread
Mustard   Mayonnaise
Pimento-stuffed Olives
Coffee   Spiced Tea

Good Friends' Dessert
(approximately 20 couples)

This is good for Thanksgiving, Christmas, or Valentine's Day gatherings.
Cheeseball and Crackers
Mulled Cider   Coffee
Cola Cake   Caramel Cake
Apple Cake or Fruit Cake
Mincemeat Cookies
Peppermint Canes

Thomasville, Georgia

Ice Cream Social
(24 to 30 people)

Homemade Peppermint, Chocolate Chip,
and Vanilla Ice Cream
served in styrofoam cups
Pound Cake, Chocolate Chip Cookies, and Cola Cake

served on decorative paper plates and napkins
Water   Coffee
Dr. and Mrs. William King
Mr. and Mrs. James R. Neill
Mr. and Mrs. Paul Hjort

Neighborhood or Church Group Fish Fry

Mullet with Hush Puppies
Slaw   Pickles
Grits (optional)
Lemon Dessert   Tea or Coffee
Thomasville, Georgia

Wassail Party

Thanksgiving, Christmas, New Year's

Wassail
Hot Roast Beef   Party Rolls
Cheeseball   Crackers
Crabmeat Dip with Fresh Vegetables
Cauliflower, cucumber, yellow squash,
Zucchini, celery, carrot strips, radish
Fresh Fruit Bowl
Melon balls, fresh pineapple chunks,
Sliced bananas, strawberries

or

Strawberries with powdered sugar for dipping
Bite-size Fruit Cakes or Fruit Cake Cookies
Ella Moore

Candlelight Dessert

Chocolate Delight
Strawberry Cake
Italian Cream Cake
Fruit and nuts for dunking in Chocolate Fondue
Banana Punch   Coffee
Cascile and Malcolm Knight

The Selfs' Christmas Open House

Spritz Decorated Cookies
Pickups
Pound Cake cut in rectangles
Cheese and Crackers   Nuts
Easy Punch   Coffee

The Bill Kings' Traditional Christmas Eve Dinner
(about 12 people)

Country-Cured Ham (17 pounds)   Consommé Rice
Cold Fresh Applesauce
Canned Cranberry Sauce
Strawberry Congealed Salad
Sectional Grapefruit-Asparagus Salad
Duncan Hines Blueberry Muffins
Water   Fruit Cake
Hot Chocolate   Coffee

The Bill Kings' Traditional Christmas Day Dinner

Turkey (fast method)   Dressing
Lime Salad or Sunshine Salad
Cranberry Sauce
Small Butterbeans or Broccoli Puff
Rice and Gravy   Angel Biscuits
Coffee

New Year's Day Dinner

Pork Roast   Baked Sweet Potatoes
Black-eyed Peas (cooked in ham hock)
Turnip Greens   Cornbread
Cherry Cobbler

Norma and Bill Key

Finger Foods, Dips, and Spreads

Cheese Biscuits

½ pound butter (room temp.)
½ pound sharp cheese (room temp.)
1 tablespoon salt
2 teaspoons sugar
2 cups flour
Paprika and red pepper to taste

Cream butter and cheese. Mix other ingredients. Roll out on floured board to ½ inch thick. Cut with small cutter. Bake at 360 degrees until *lightly* browned (15 to 20 minutes). Good for coffees.

Mrs. William King (originally
Stegall family recipe)

Cheese Crackers

2 cups flour
2 cups Rice Krispies
2 cups sharp cheese
2 sticks butter or margarine
½ teaspoon salt
½ teaspoon red pepper

Mix all ingredients together and form into several long rolls. Chill. Slice and place slices on cookie sheet. Bake at 375 degrees until lightly browned.

Helen Allen

Cheese Olive Hors d'Oeuvres

60 stuffed olives, well drained
2 cups grated sharp cheddar cheese
½ cup butter
1 cup flour
½ teaspoon salt
1 teaspoon paprika

Blend cheese with butter. Sift together flour, salt and paprika. Add to cheese mixture and mix well. Pinch off a small amount of the dough, flatten in the palm of your hand, and wrap the dough around each olive. Freeze. Do not thaw before baking. When ready to bake, place cheeseballs on baking sheet and bake in a preheated 400-degree over for 15 minutes. Makes about 5 dozen.

Lealice Dehoney

Cheese Rounds

1 stick butter or margarine
2 cups grated sharp cheese (½ pound)
1 cup flour
1 teaspoon salt
Tabasco or red pepper to taste
Pecans

Let butter and cheese stand until soft. Mix butter, cheese, salt, and Tabasco with hands gradually adding flour. Divide into about three parts and work into long rolls in wax paper. Chill in refrigerator. Slice thin; put pecan on top. Bake on ungreased cookie sheet at 350 degrees for about 15 minutes. Allow to brown slightly. Makes about 100. These freeze beautifully and are good for teas and coffees.

Lucille Herron

Cheese Sticks

1 stick (½ cup) very soft butter
½ pound sharp cheese, grated, very soft
2 cups flour, unsifted
1 teaspoon salt
3 dashes cayenne pepper

With a fork combine softened butter and cheese. Into this sift flour, salt, and pepper. *Mix well* with hands. Place in cookie press with star tip. Turn out on ungreased cookie sheet. Place in preheated 325-degree oven, then reduce to 300 degrees and bake 20 minutes. Makes 80 to 100 cheese sticks.

Mrs. W. R. Thomas, Jr.

Cheese Straws

1 cup plain flour	3 tablespoons cold water
1 cup grated sharp cheese	Dash cayenne pepper
1 stick margarine	½ teaspoon baking powder

Mix cheese and margarine. Add flour which has been mixed with baking powder and cayenne pepper. Mix well. Add water and mix. Put in cookie press and press into straws. Bake at 350-degrees for 10 to 12 minutes. Store in airtight container.

Polly Pledger

Easy Hors d'oeuvres

For quick pizzas which we use cut in small wedges for hors d'oeuvres, try the Arab bread found in supermarket, using your favorite pizza fixings. Just split the bread making two pizzas from one round piece. Smear the goodies on top of each and heat in the oven until all the cheese is melted and the edges of the bread pastry are beginning to curl and get crunchy.

Doty Bean

Calico Cheeseball

½ pound grated sharp cheddar cheese
1 (8-ounce) package cream cheese
½ cup chopped nuts
¼ cup chopped stuffed olives or
   1 small can crushed pineapple, drained
Dash salt
¼ cup chopped green pepper
¼ cup mayonnaise

Mix all ingredients and roll into two balls or a log. Serve with crackers or Melba toast.

Norma and Bill Key

Sausage Balls

1 pound ground sausage	**½ teaspoon ginger**
½ cup catsup	**½ cup dark brown sugar**
½ cup wine vinegar	**Dash salt**
1 tablespoon soy sauce	

Roll sausage into balls and cook. Combine remaining ingredients to make sauce. Put sausage balls in sauce at least one hour before serving. Serve in chafing dish to keep warm.

Norma and Bill Key

Sausage Balls

2 cups Bisquick	**1 pound hot ground sausage**
1 cup grated cheese	

Mix together ingredients and form into bite-size balls. Bake at 325 degrees for 25 minutes.

Ella Moore

Cheese and Sausage Balls

1 pound sharp cheddar cheese, grated
1 pound hot ground sausage
3 cups Bisquick

Mix ingredients together well. Roll into small balls. Bake at 375 degrees for 10 to 12 minutes.

Mrs. Paul Hjort

Sherry Cheese Paté

6 ounces cream cheese
1 cup grated sharp cheddar cheese
4 teaspoons sherry
½ teaspoon curry powder
¼ teaspoon salt
½ cup mango chutney
⅓ cup finely chopped green onions with tops

Mix cream cheese, cheddar cheese, sherry, curry, and salt until mixture is smooth. Spread in round or flat plate and chill until firm. Cover top with chutney and onions.

Norma and Bill Key

How to Make Rolled Sandwiches

Mr. Charles Wood at Sky Valley taught me how to make rolled finger sandwiches. It is very similar to the description given by Janis Kelly in the Rolled Sandwich recipe.

1. Remove all crusts.

2. On breadboard flatten bread lightly with rolling pin.

3. For putting two pieces (overlap) of bread together, butter the ends where seam will be and flatten one on top of the other.

4. Spread bread with salad dressing, mayonnaise, or cream cheese mixed with sour cream.

5. Place pineapple strip, asparagus spear, or whatever you desire and roll up jelly roll fashion.

6. Seal with butter on overlap.

7. Chill thoroughly. Slice to desired thickness for finger sandwiches.

Bar-B-Burgers

1 pound hamburger
1 small onion cut fine
1 green pepper cut fine
2 tablespoons margarine
2 tablespoons sugar
1 tablespoon Worcestershire sauce
½ cup catsup
½ cup chili sauce
1 teaspoon mustard
1 teaspoon salt
1 tablespoon chili powder

Brown meat, onion, and green pepper in margarine. Add remaining ingredients. Refrigerate and use later. Heat and serve on hot hamburger buns.

Frances Moore

Chipped Beef Sandwiches

2 (8-ounce) packages cream cheese, softened
2 packages chipped beef
1 bell pepper
1 tablespoon onion

½ **cup celery**
Mayonnaise
Parsley for garnish

Chop beef, onion, celery, and pepper on medium blade of food chopper. Add cheese and enough mayonnaise to make spreading consistency and mix well. Make open-faced circles garnished with parsley, closed tiny triangles, or ribbon sandwiches. If you make these the night before a tea, the best way to keep them moist is to line a small dress box with aluminum foil and layer the sandwiches with strips of wax paper between. Over the top layer of wax paper place a damp tea towel and then seal with foil. Refrigerate.

Janis Kelly

Fried Boneless Breast of Chicken on Seeded Buns

Preheat deep fryer to 325 degrees or use a large heavy skillet with about 1 inch of cooking oil heated to 325 degrees. Remove skin and bone from chicken breasts and divide into halves (8 pieces). Dry each piece carefully.

Method 1:

4 chicken breasts	**Cooking oil**
1 cup flour	**Buttermilk**
1 teaspoon salt	**8 seeded buns**
½ **teaspoon pepper**	

Soak the chicken breasts in buttermilk for at least 1 hour. Drain and dust well with flour (shake chicken in a paper sack with flour, salt, and pepper). Place in hot oil and turn to brown on all sides. Cook for about 20 minutes or until it feels tender with a fork. Remove from pan; drain on paper towels. Place each piece in a seeded bun and wrap in plastic wrap.

Method 2:

4 chicken breasts	**1 teaspoon pepper**
3 eggs	**1 cup slivered almonds**
1 teaspoon salt	**8 seeded buns**

Beat together eggs, salt, and pepper. Dip chicken pieces in beaten eggs, and then roll in slivered almonds. Place in hot oil and turn to brown on all sides. Cook for about 20 minutes or until tender. Remove from pan, drain excess grease on paper towels. Place each piece in a seeded bun and wrap in plastic wrap.

Betty Van Gerpen

Cucumber Sandwiches

Bread, white and brown	**Cucumbers**
Mayonnaise	**Paprika**

Cut bread into small circles. Spread lightly with mayonnaise and store in a container in the refrigerator until the day of the party. Peel cucumbers and slice ⅛ inch thick. Place a slice of cucumber on a bread circle and sprinkle with paprika.

Mrs. Paul Hjort

Open-faced Tomato Sandwiches

Bread	**Cherry tomatoes**
Mayonnaise	**Salt and pepper**

Cut bread rounds the day before the party. Spread mayonnaise on rounds and put two together, mayonnaise sides facing. Place in layers in an airtight plastic container, each layer covered with wax paper. The tomatoes may also be cut in slices the night before the party and put in a separate container. A few minutes before the party, separate the bread rounds, place a slice of tomato on each, and sprinkle with salt and pepper.

Mrs. Talbot Nunnally

Rolled Sandwiches

Bread, thin sliced	**Garlic salt**
Cream cheese	**Midget kosher dill pickles**
Mayonnaise or cream	**Pickled okra**
Green food coloring	

Soften cream cheese and thin with a small amount of mayonnaise or cream. Tint light green. Add a little garlic salt if desired. Remove the crusts from the bread and flatten slices lightly with a rolling pin. Spread each slice with the cream cheese mixture and place on each a row of pickles or okra. Roll up jelly roll fashion. Place seam side down and refrigerate (covered well) until serving time. When ready to serve, slice each roll into 4 or 5 small rolled sandwiches.

Janis Kelly

Vegetable Sandwich

1 envelope gelatin
1 pint mayonnaise
1 cup celery, chopped
1 small onion, chopped
2 tomatoes, seeded and chopped
1 green pepper, seeded and chopped
1 cucumber, seeded and chopped

Soften gelatin in ¼ cup cold water, then dissolve mixture in ¼ cup boiling water. Cool. Fold in 1 pint mayonnaise and add remaining ingredients. Place in refrigerator for several hours. Make up sandwiches (with mayonnaise) and cut into party size. This mixture can be made a day or more ahead. Guaranteed to be completely consumed, no matter how many you make.

Norma and Bill Key

Hush Puppies

1 cup water-ground corn meal
½ teaspoon double-acting baking powder
½ teaspoon salt
1 teaspoon sugar
2 tablespoons minced onion
1 egg
¼ cup buttermilk

Mix together first five ingredients and then add egg and buttermilk. Form into finger-shaped patties or drop from a spoon into deep fat at 370 degrees. Fry until golden brown. Drain on absorbent paper and keep warm till serving.

Hush Puppies

1 cup cornmeal mix	1 egg
1 teaspoon sugar	¼ cup buttermilk
2 tablespoons minced onion	

Mix all ingredients together. Form into finger-shaped patties or drop from a spoon into deep fat. Fry at 370 degrees until golden brown. Drain on absorbent paper and keep warm until serving.

Carolyn Self

Clam Dip

1½ cups (12-ounce carton) creamed cottage cheese
¾ cup (8-ounce can) drained minced clams
1 teaspoon salt
⅛ teaspoon pepper
1 teaspoon lemon juice
1 teaspoon Worcestershire sauce
1 teaspoon chili sauce
Dash Tabasco sauce
Dash paprika

In blender, process cottage cheese at high speed until creamy, scraping sides of blender often. Add remaining ingredients except paprika. Process at medium speed until thoroughly combined. Pour into small bowl; sprinkle with paprika. Chill before serving. Makes 1¾ cups of dip.

Irma Spearman

Dip Appetizer

1 (8-ounce) package cream cheese
2 tablespoons milk
1 (2½-ounce) package dried beef, finely chopped
2 tablespoons minced onion
2 tablespoons chopped green pepper
⅛ teaspoon pepper
½ cup sour cream
¼ cup chopped nuts

Warm all ingredients in double boiler until well mixed. Serve with crackers.

Norma and Bill Key

Vegetable Dip

1 cup plain yogurt
1 teaspoon instant minced onion
½ teaspoon salt
¼ teaspoon dill weed
¼ teaspoon leaf oregano
⅛ teaspoon garlic salt
⅛ teaspoon pepper
2 teaspoons sugar

Place all ingredients in blender or mixer. Using medium speed, process until smooth and well blended. Refrigerate overnight. A good dressing for tossed salad.

Lealice Dehoney

Sandwich Spread

1 (8-ounce) package cream cheese
¾ cup chopped nuts
¼ cup chopped green pepper
¼ cup chopped onion
3 tablespoons chopped pimento
1 tablespoon catsup
3 hard cooked eggs, finely chopped
¾ tablespoon salt
Dash pepper

Soften cream cheese and add other ingredients.

Mrs. Rudolph Davis

Mrs. Donaldson's Ham Salad Spread

2 cups finely chopped ham
¾ cup chopped celery
1 teaspoon chopped onion
¼ teaspoon Tabasco
½ teaspoon Worcestershire sauce
Dash salt and pepper
Salad dressing (Durkee's)

Ham may be chopped in the blender. Mix all ingredients together and add enough salad dressing (not mayonnaise) to make spreading consistency.

Crabmeat Dip

1 (8-ounce) package cream cheese
1 (6½-ounce) can crabmeat
2 tablespoons chopped onion
½ teaspoon creamy horseradish
1 tablespoon milk
¼ teaspoon salt
⅛ teaspoon pepper
⅓ cup toasted sliced almonds

Mix all ingredients except almonds, and spoon into glass baking dishes. Bake at 375 degrees for 15 minutes. Put into chafing dish. Serve with raw vegetables, such as zucchini, crooked neck squash, cucumbers, carrots, celery, and cauliflower.

Irma Spearman
Ella Moore

Soups and Salads

Cream of Peanut Soup

½ cup butter
1 cup celery, finely chopped
1 medium onion, minced
2 tablespoons all-purpose flour
2 quarts chicken both
1 cup creamy style peanut butter
1 cup light cream or half-and-half (optional)
¼ cup snipped parsley
¼ cup coarsely chopped salted peanuts

Early in the day in a 3- or 4-quart saucepan melt butter. Add celery and onion and cook until lightly browned. Stir in flour and blend well. Gradually stir in chicken broth and bring to a boil. Stir in peanut butter and simmer about 15 minutes. Place in refrigerator. Before serving, reheat to serving temperature. Stir in cream if desired. Serve in tureen or cups, topping each with peanuts and parsley.

Chili

1 medium onion, chopped
1 medium green pepper, chopped
1 pound ground beef
2 cans chili beans
1 can tomatoes
1 can tomato soup
1 tablespoon chili powder
Bacon grease

Sauté onion and pepper in bacon grease until tender. Add ground beef and brown. Add remaining ingredients and simmer 1 hour. Serves 4.

Frances Moore

Gazpacho Andaluz (Blender Method)

Blend together for 2 or 3 minutes:

1 cup pared cucumber
1 small jar pimentos, drained
2 cups skinned tomatoes
1 small onion, peeled and halved
⅓ cup salad oil
½ cup green pepper
½ (16-ounce) can tomato juice
⅓ cup red wine vinegar
¼ cup Tobasco
1½ teaspoons salt
⅛ teaspoon black pepper
1 clove of garlic, split (optional)

Pour into large bowl and add:

1½ (16-ounce) cans tomato juice
¼ cup chopped chives

Mix well by stirring. Cover bowl and refrigerate until well chilled (about 2 hours). Chill 6 serving bowls. Prepare garnish of finely chopped cucumber, onion, and green pepper (about ¼ cup of each). Brown about 2 cups croutons. Serve croutons and garnishes as accompaniments.

Bettie Holley

Strawberry Soup

2 cups fresh strawberries   2 cups ice water
½ cup sugar   ½ cup red wine
½ cup sour cream

Crush berries in blender. Add sugar and sour cream and mix well. Then add water and wine. Mix and chill. Makes 6 small servings.

Frances Moore

Asparagus Vinaigrette with Water Chestnuts

Italian Wishbone dressing
1 (15-ounce) can asparagus

¼ cup pimento snips
1 small can water chestnuts, thinly sliced

Marinate ingredients in dressing overnight. Use enough dressing to cover ingredients. To serve, drain vegetables carefully.

Betty Van Gerpen

Frozen Cherry-Pineapple Salad

1 can cherry pie filling
1 (9-ounce) can crushed pineapple, drained
⅓ cup lemon juice
1 (14-ounce) can condensed milk
1 large container whipped topping
1 cup pecans

Combine all ingredients. Pour into square glass baking dish (or milk carton) and freeze.

Lealice Dehoney

Chicken Salad

3 cups chicken, cooked and cubed
½ cup celery, thinly sliced
2 hard-boiled eggs, chopped
1 large red Delicious apple, cored and cubed
½ cup water chestnuts, sliced (optional)
½ cup mayonnaise
½ cup sour cream
2 teaspoons prepared yellow mustard

Toss all ingredients lightly. Serves 8.

Ella Moore

Chicken Salad

1 stewing chicken (4 to 5 pounds)
1 rib celery
1 slice onion
1 small can water chestnuts, chopped
1 cup celery, chopped

1 teaspoon grated onion
2 hard-boiled eggs, chopped
½ to ¾ cup mayonnaise, or enough to moisten
Salt and pepper to taste
1 cup peacans, chopped (optional)

Simmer chicken in salted water with rib of celery and slice of onion until tender. Cool. Cut chicken in small chunks. Add remaining ingredients.

Frances Moore

Cold Bean Salad

1 (8-ounce) can green beans
1 can yellow wax beans
1 can kidney beans
1 rib celery, chopped
1 bell pepper, chopped
1 onion, sliced thin

½ cup sugar
½ cup cider vinegar
½ cup salad oil
1 teaspoon salt
½ teaspoon black pepper

Combine beans, celery, pepper, and onion; set aside. Combine sugar and vinegar in saucepan and bring to a boil. Remove from heat and cool. Add oil, salt, and pepper to sugar and vinegar mixture; combine with remaining ingredients. Cover salad and refrigerate overnight. Drain before serving. Serves 8.

Frances Moore

Congealed Black Cherry Salad

1 large package black cherry gelatin
1 (20-ounce) can crushed pineapple, drained
1 (16-ounce) can black cherries
1 cup nuts, chopped
2 cups boiling water
Mayonnaise

Dissolve gelatin in boiling water. Add remaining ingredients and pour into molds. Refrigerate until congealed or overnight. Serve on lettuce with mayonnaise.

Frances Moore

Congealed Lime Salad

2 small packages lime gelatin
2 cups boiling water
1 large package cream cheese, softened
1 large can crushed pineapple
¾ cup small marshmallows
1 cup chopped pecans

Drain pineapple and reserve juice. Dissolve gelatin in 2 cups boiling water. Add cream cheese. Dissolve. Add drained pineapple plus approximately ¾ cup pineapple juice. Allow marshmallows to almost completely dissolve. Add nuts. Place in slightly greased mold and refrigerate. (For Christmas I use Tupperware mold with Christmas tree or star insert.)

Anne King from Mrs. Ramsey

Peach Pickle Salad

1 large jar peach pickles, cut up
1 cup diced celery
½ cup chopped nuts
1 package lemon gelatin
1 cup peach juice
1 cup boiling water

Dissolve gelatin in 3 cups boiling water. Add 1 cup peach juice. Add pickles, nuts, and celery. Pour into mold and congeal.

Mrs. Tom Vann, Jr.

Picnic Style Creamed Potatoes

4 cups cooked, cubed potatoes
1 quart salad dressing
1 large can evaporated milk
½ cup sugar
3 tablespoons prepared mustard
4 hard-boiled eggs, sliced
1 small onion, chopped (optional)
Olives
Parsley

Peel and cube potatoes and cook until done but not mushy. Drain and refrigerate. Combine salad dressing, evaporated milk, sugar, and mustard and beat well; refrigerate. When ready to serve, combine potatoes, eggs, onions, and olives. Add enough salad dressing to make right consistency. Serve in individual plastic containers (with lid) with parsley spring on top. Serves approximately 8.

Author's note: The salad dressing which is left over is delicious used as a sauce for hot vegetables and as a dressing for tossed salad.

Betty Van Gerpen

Potato Salad

3 Irish potatoes
½ cup chopped celery
2 hard-boiled eggs
1 small onion, finely chopped
2 tablespoons sweet pickle relish
2 tablespoons pimento, chopped
2 tablespoons green pepper, chopped
Mayonnaise
1 teaspoon dry mustard
¾ teaspoon salt

Peel and cube potatoes and cook in small amount of water with ¾ teaspoon salt just until tender. Drain. Add all other ingredients except mayonnaise and dry mustard. Add enough mayonnaise to moisten and hold together. Add mustard. Serves 4.

Frances Moore

Strawberry Congealed Salad

2 small packages strawberry gelatin
2 cups boiling water
2 small packages frozen strawberries
1½ cups crushed pineapple, drained
2 large bananas, sliced (optional)
1 cup sour cream

Dissolve gelatin in water. Add berries, pineapple, and

bananas. Pour half in oblong casserole. Chill until firm. Leave the remaining half in the bowl and chill to thickness of egg whites, then remove from refrigerator. If you are afraid you will forget and let it congeal, just leave it out of the refrigerator. Spoon sour cream over congealed gelatin, spread evenly, and cover with remainder of gelatin mixture. Congeal. This is a favorite of children.

Mrs. Glenn Wright, Jr.
Mrs. Bill King

Sunshine Salad

2 small packages strawberry gelatin
2 cups boiling water
1 cup cold water
1 can fruit cocktail, drained
½ cup pineapple juice
1 small can crushed pineapple
1 cup small marshmallows (optional)
½ cup nuts, chopped
¼ cup sugar
2 teaspoons flour
¼ cup pineapple juice
1 egg
1 tablespoon margarine
1 envelope whipped topping

Dissolve gelatin in boiling water. Add cold water. Add fruit cocktail, crushed pineapple, marshmallows, nuts, and the ½ cup pineapple juice. Congeal until set. Combine sugar, flour, the ¼ cup pineapple juice, egg, and margarine. Cook over medium heat until thick, stirring constantly. Cool. Prepare whipped topping according to package directions and fold into cooled mixture. Spread on salad.

Mrs. Charles McDaniel
Anne King

Tomatoes/Asparagus

2 to 3 large ripe tomatoes (or enough for 8 nice slices)
16 asparagus spears
8 (1-inch) strips pimento

½ **cup mayonnaise**
1 tablespoon lemon juice
Paprika

Place 2 asparagus spears on each tomato slice. Dot with dressing made with mayonnaise and lemon juice. Top with pimento strip and paprika. May be served hot by placing under broiler until heated.

Ella Moore

Grapefruit Asparagus Salad

Alternate sections of grapefruit with asparagus spears on a bed of greens. Serve with side dish of French dressing. Both grapefruit and asparagus can be canned, which makes a very quick salad. Slices of pimento can be added to give color.

Anne King

Meats & Poultry

Chuck Roast Cut-Up

1 roast
1 can golden mushroom soup
1 can onion soup
Additional mushrooms if desired

Put roast in crock pot. Add soups which have been mixed together. Add additional mushrooms, if desired. Cook all day on low.

Nanci Simmons

Flank Steak London Broil

1½ to 2 pounds flank steak
¾ cup red wine vinegar
¾ cup vegetable oil
¼ cup Worcestershire sauce
1 teaspoon garlic salt
1 teaspoon thyme
1 medium sliced onion

Mix marinade ingredients in flat pan or dish and add the steak. Marinate several hours if time permits, but steak can be cooked in 30 minutes. Cook on grill 5 minutes each side for rare. Slice thin.

Nanci Simmons

London Broil

1 (1¾ pounds) flank steak
1 teaspoon salt
1 clove garlic, mashed
½ onion, chopped

½ teaspoon black pepper   1 tablespoon wine vinegar
¼ teaspoon basil   2 tablespoons salad oil
¼ teaspoon Rosemary

Combine all ingredients except steak in shallow glass pan. Brush both sides of steak with marinade. Let stand in mixture two hours. Broil 3 inches from heat for 5 minutes. Turn, brush with marinade, and broil another 4 minutes. Slice steak diagonally across grain, as thin as possible. Spoon pan juices over meat. Serves 4 to 6.

Frances Moore

Marinated Shish Kabobs

Round steak or fillet of beef, cut in cubes
Instant marinade (or your favorite marinade recipe)
Cherry tomatoes
Mushrooms
Tiny onions
Rice, cooked in beef bouillon

Cut meat in cubes and remove all fat. Marinate meat. On small skewers (about 4 to 5 inches long), alternate meat, tomatoes, mushrooms, and onions, placing meat between each vegetable. Use marinade as sauce to cook the shish kabob in. Wrap skewers in aluminum foil (or use cooking bag) and bake until meat is tender or to your liking. Plan on serving 2 shish kabobs for each guest. Serve with rice. This is easy and an interesting change from the usual fare. Round steak should be marinated longer for greater tenderness.

Carolyn Self

Roast Pork Tenderloin

3 pounds whole pork tenderloin
½ cup soy sauce
1 tablespoon grated onion
2 shakes garlic salt
Bacon strips
1 tablespoon wine vinegar
¼ teaspoon pepper
½ teaspoon sugar

Mix sauce by combining soy sauce, onion, garlic salt, vinegar, pepper, and sugar. Place tenderloin in shallow pan or baking dish and marinate in sauce for 2 to 3 hours. Roll tenderloin in sauce occasionally. Pour off liquid and use to baste meat while cooking. Place bacon strips across loin. Bake in 300 degree oven for 1¾ hours. Serves 6.

Norma and Bill Key

Fried Fish
Mullet, Trout, or Bream

Wash cleaned fish and dry thoroughly. Cover with corn meal. Fry 5 to 7 minutes on each side in 1 inch of hot oil. Small fish may be fried whole. Larger fish should be boned and cut in fillets before they are fried. Sprinkle each side with salt and pepper as they cook. Turn only once to avoid having the fish fall apart. Use a large heavy skillet.

Cooking fish over a fire or gas grill is the best way. The odor is hard to get rid of indoors. To remove fish odors, wash your hands in cold tea.

Carolyn Self

Crab Bake

¼ cup butter
4 tablespoons flour
2 cups milk
½ teaspoon pepper
¾ cup (or more) dry bread crumbs, buttered generously
1 pound can crab meat
1 small jar pimento, chopped
½ cup blanched slivered almonds (optional)

Melt butter; add flour and bread. Add milk and cook until thick, stirring constantly. Add pepper, crab meat, pimento, and nuts. Pour into greased molds or into 1½-quart greased casserole. Top with buttered bread crumbs (or crushed Ritz crackers). Bake at 325 degrees for 20 to 25 minutes. Can be made ahead and refrigerated until time to bake. Good for buffet with sliced ham or ham, biscuits, and asparagus, etc. Serves 8.

Carolyn Self

"Self-Style" Neufchâtel Fondue

3 cups dry white or rosé wine
2 teaspoons lemon juice
4 cups grated Gruyère cheese
4 cups grated natural Swiss cheese
4 tablespoons flour, heated in a little wine
Day-old French bread
Tiny sausages
Olives
Shrimp
Tiny pickles

Spray inside of fondue pot with vegetable spray-on. Spray a big boiler with vegetable spray-on to make the whole recipe at one time. A fondue pot is too small. Heat wine and lemon juice carefully in large boiler and gradually add (stirring constantly) cheese and flour mixed in warm wine until smooth and creamy. Divide mixture into two fondue pots and place on *low* to medium heat until ready for use. Keep stirring with wooden spoon from bottom, making a figure eight. If during meal fondue gets too thick, thin *very* gradually with white wine. If, heaven forbid, the fondue curdles, add a few drops of lemon juice and stir vigorously.

After you do this a few times, it becomes simple. Practice a few times on your family before undertaking a party. Use day-old French bread cut in cubes. Leave the crust on. Spear the bread, dip, and make figure-eight motion. Be careful; it will burn your tongue. Also provide for dipping: tiny sausages, olives, shrimp, tiny pickles, cooked sliced carrot—whatever you imagine. Serves 8.

The Self's Favorite Beef Fondue

Filet of beef or round steak	Cooking oil
Instant marinade	Meat sauces
Meat tenderizer	

You may use filet of beef cut in 1-inch cubes or for a more economical meal round steak marinated with tenderizer. The flavor is better no matter which you use if you marinate the meat. Use your favorite marinade plus tenderizer. Sometimes I use instant marinade or mix my own using soy sauce, Worcestershire, a little burgundy wine, and lemon pepper. Do not add salt when using soy sauce. Remove all fat from the meat. Use six to eight ounces of beef per person. We like to use peanut oil best, but any cooking oil will be fine.

Fill fondue pot to just under half full, heat to very hot (test for sizzle), and regulate burner as needed. The meat takes only a few minutes to cook (depending on the taste of the individual). Dip in your favorite sauce and enjoy!

Chicken Breast Supreme

8 chicken breasts (boned halves)
8 strips bacon
2 (2½-ounce) jars dried beef
½ pint sour cream
1 can mushroom soup
1 can milk
1 can mushrooms, drained
Black pepper to taste; add no salt

Wrap each breast with a bacon strip. Place in baking dish lined with two layers of beef. Blend sour cream, soup, and milk; add drained mushrooms and black pepper. Pour over chicken. Bake 3 hours in 300-degree oven. May be cooked ahead and reheated at serving time. This is a good recipe to double.

Nanci Simmons

Chicken Breasts with Peaches

2 chicken breasts, split
Salt and pepper
¼ cup butter or margarine
¼ cup minced green onion
1 clove garlic, minced
1 teaspoon paprika
1 bunch broccoli, cooked
4 canned peach halves
1 cup sour cream
¼ cup mayonnaise
¼ cup grated Parmesan cheese

Season chicken with salt and pepper. Melt butter. Add onion and garlic. Sauté. Add paprika and turn chicken in mixture until coated. Put in shallow baking dish. Cover loosely and bake for 20 minutes at 375 degrees. Arrange drained broccoli in pan beside chicken. Put peaches in pan. Mix sour cream and mayonnaise and spoon over all. Sprinkle with cheese; put low in broiler and broil 6 to 8 minutes until glazed and richly flecked with brown.

Lealice Dehoney

Chicken Casserole

2 cups diced chicken	½ teaspoon salt
1 can cream of chicken soup	½ cup almonds
2 tablespoons chopped onion	¾ cup mayonnaise
1 cup chopped celery	3 teaspoons lemon juice
1 cup cooked rice	Crushed potato chips

Combine all ingredients except potato chips. Put crushed potato chips on top. Bake at 375 degrees for 30 minutes. This can be frozen.

Ginny Osburn

Chicken Curry

6 tablespoons butter or margarine
1½ cups diagonally sliced celery
1 medium onion, minced
6 tablespoons flour
1 teaspoon salt
Dash of pepper
3 cups milk
1 can undiluted cream of mushroom soup
2 cups diced cooked ham
2 cups diced cooked chicken
2 tablespoons minced pimento
1½ teaspoons curry powder
Cooked rice
Curry accompaniments such as grated hard-boiled eggs, crumbled crisp bacon, coconut, peanuts, chutney

Melt butter in large skillet and sauté onion and celery until tender. Stir in flour, salt, and pepper; then add milk. Cook, stirring constantly until sauce is thickened. Add soup, ham, chicken, pimento, and curry powder. Turn into 2-quart casserole. Bake uncovered at 350 degrees for 1 hour. Serve immediately on a bed of rice.

Put grated hard-boiled eggs, crumbled crisp bacon, peanuts, coconut, and chutney on separate dishes. Each person can put the combination desired on top of the curry.

Frances Moore

Chicken Divan

1 (3-pound) fryer
1 large bunch fresh broccoli or 2 packages frozen
2 chicken bouillon cubes, dissolved in 2 cups hot water
4 tablespoons flour
½ cup evaporated skimmed milk, undiluted
3 tablespoons cooking sherry
Salt, pepper
Grated cheese

Wrap chicken in aluminum foil and bake in 325-degree oven about 2 hours. Cook broccoli in boiling water until tender; drain and set aside.

Make sauce by using ¼ cup chicken bouillon with flour. Blend in saucepan over low heat; gradually add remaining 1¾ cups bouillon, stirring constantly until thick and smooth. Cook over low heat about 10 minutes, stirring frequently. Remove from heat and fold in evaporated milk, which has been whipped. (To whip evaporated milk, thoroughly chill the milk, bowl, and beaters.) Add sherry. Season to taste with salt and pepper.

Remove chicken from bone and alternate meat with broccoli and sauce, beginning with broccoli and topping with chicken. Cover with remaining sauce and sprinkle with grated cheese. Place under broiler until sauce bubbles and is lightly browned. Serves 6.

Ella Moore

Chicken Tetrazzini

2 whole chickens (large fryers)
1 (16-ounce) package noodles
2 cans mushroom soup
10 ounces sharp cheese, grated
1 large onion
1 small jar pimento
1 small can mushrooms
1 small can pitted olives
Salt, pepper and Worcestershire sauce to taste
1 package slivered almonds (optional)

Cook chicken covered in water until done. Cool; remove chicken from bones and cut in bite-size pieces. Reserve 1½ cups stock. Cook noodles in remaining stock (you may need to add water). Combine all ingredients including reserved liquid. Bake in two large, greased casseroles. Bake 20 to 25 minutes in 350-degree oven. Serves 18 to 20.

Mrs. Tom Vann, Jr.

Herbed Chicken Bake

1 (6-ounce) package long-grain wild rice mix
3 large chicken breasts, boned and halved
¼ cup butter or margarine
1 (10½-ounce) can cream of chicken soup
¾ cup sauterne
½ cup sliced celery
1 (3-ounce) can sliced mushrooms, drained
2 tablespoons chopped canned pimento
Salt and pepper

Heat over to 350 degrees. Prepare rice mix using package directions. Season chicken with salt and pepper. Brown slowly in skillet, in butter. Spoon rice into 1½-quart casserole, top with chicken, skin side up. Add soup to skillet; slowly add sauterne, stirring until smooth. Add remaining ingredients; bring to boil; pour over chicken. Cover. Bake for 25 minutes. Uncover and bake 15 to 20 minutes more or until tender. Serves 6.

Kathy Dehoney

Holiday Chicken Casserole

1 (4 to 5 pounds) hen or 2 fryers
1 (8-ounce) package spaghetti
1 can cream of mushroom soup
1 can cream of celery soup
1 small can pimentos
1 small can mushrooms

Half cover the chicken with salted water (simmer until very tender). Remove chicken and cut into small pieces. About 1 hour before serving, bring broth to a boil and add spaghetti. Cook until tender; do not drain off liquid. Add mushroom and celery soups and shredded pimento and mushrooms. Add diced chicken. Turn into casserole and bake in moderate oven just long enough to heat thoroughly. Serves 12.

Lealice Dehoney

Chicken and Wild Rice Casserole

1 cup wild rice
½ cup chopped onion
1 stick butter or margarine
¼ cup flour
1 (6-ounce) can mushrooms
1 cup sour cream
3 cups cooked chicken, diced
¼ cup diced pimento
2 tablespoons parsley
1 cup chicken broth
½ cup slivered blanched almonds
Salt and pepper

Prepare rice according to directions. Cook onion in butter until tender but not brown. Remove from heat, stir in flour. Stir broth into flour mixture, add sour cream and cook, stirring constantly, until thick. Add rice, mushrooms, chicken, pimento, parsley, salt, and pepper. Place in 2-quart casserole. Sprinkle with almonds. Bake at 350 degrees for 25 to 30 minutes. Serves 8.

Wynelle MacMullen

Turkey Casserole

1 cup turkey, cooked and chopped
1 cup celery
½ cup mayonnaise
1 can cream of mushroom soup
1 teaspoon grated onion
2 hard-boiled eggs, chopped
Tabasco sauce
Worcestershire sauce
Salt
Dried bread crumbs

Mix together turkey, celery, mayonnaise, soup, onion, and eggs. Add Tabasco sauce, Worcestershire sauce, and salt to taste. Top with bread crumbs and bake at 350 degrees until hot and bubbly (about 40 minutes). Serves 6.

Lealice Dehoney

Turkey (Fast Bake)

Wash bird. Stuff with 2 small onions, 2 ribs celery (with leaves). Sprinkle bird inside and outside with salt and pepper and ¼ cup melted margarine. Place on back on long sheet of heavy-duty aluminum foil. Put small folds of foil over wing tips and ends of drumsticks to prevent puncturing. Bring ends of foil up, overlapping 3 inches on breast of bird. Use another piece of foil going in opposite direction. Wrap bird loosely and place in shallow pan, breast up in preheated 450-degree oven. For extra-large birds you will want to add more onions and celery ribs. This is always moist and retains juices. (Author's note: It is not necessary to use onions.)

10 to 13 pounds	2¾ to 3 hours
14 to 17 pounds	3 to 3¼ hours
18 to 21 pounds	3¼ to 3½ hours
22 to 24 pounds	3½ to 3¾ hours

Anne King

Vegetables

Apples and Carrots Casserole

2 (20-ounce) cans sliced apples, undrained
3 cups carrots, cooked and sliced
Butter or margarine
¼ cup brown sugar
¾ cup sugar
4 tablespoons flour
¼ teaspoon salt
Cinnamon
Nutmeg

Place 1 can of the apples and apple liquid in buttered casserole. Cover with carrots. Dot with margarine or butter. Combine both sugars, flour, and salt. Sprinkle half the sugar mixture over carrots and apples and sprinkle with a little nutmeg and cinnamon. Pour remaining can of apples on top. Sprinkle with remainder of sugar mixture and a little cinnamon and nutmeg. Cook at 350 degrees for about 30 minutes or until hot and bubbly. Serves 8. Note: You may want to use less sugar mixture if it seems too sweet.

Ella Moore
Taffy Moore

Asparagus Casserole

2 large cans green asparagus
¾ cup sharp cheddar cheese, grated
1 can mushrooms, drained
2 hard-boiled eggs, sliced
2 tablespoons margarine or butter
2 tablespoons flour
1 scant cup whipping cream
Sliced almonds
Salt, pepper, paprika, and red pepper to taste

Drain the asparagus, reserving 2 tablespoons of juice. Melt butter. Add flour and reserved 2 tablespoons asparagus juice to form a paste. Remove from heat and stir in cream. Return to heat and stir constantly until thick and bubbly. Season with salt, pepper, and red pepper to taste. Add cheese, stirring constantly until cheese has melted and sauce is smooth. Add drained mushrooms. Set aside. Place 1 can of the drained asparagus in a buttered casserole dish; cover with half the hard-boiled egg slices and half the cheese sauce. Repeat layer and cover with almonds and sprinkle with paprika. Bake at 350 degrees for 20 minutes or until hot and bubbly. Serves 6 to 8.

Nanci Simmons

Baked Beans

1 can baked beans
1 teaspoon prepared mustard
1 tablespoon brown sugar
1 tablespoon tomato catsup
½ cup onions, chopped
3 bacon strips

Mix together all ingredients except bacon strips. Pour into baking dish. Place the bacon strips on top. Bake at 350 degrees for about 1 hour or until bacon is done.

Frances Moore

Broccoli Puff

1 (10-ounce) package frozen broccoli
1 can cream of mushroom soup
¼ cup mayonnaise
½ cup sharp cheese, shredded

¼ cup milk
1 beaten egg
¼ cup bread or cracker crumbs

Cook broccoli and drain thoroughly. (I use the broccoli cuts.) Place in a 10-by-6-by-1½-inch baking dish. Stir together soup and cheese. Gradually add milk, mayonnaise, and egg to soup mixture, stirring well. Pour over broccoli in baking dish. Sprinkle crumbs (I use Ritz crackers). Bake at 350 degrees for 45 minutes, until lightly browned. Serves 6 to 8.

Taffy Moore

Curried Fruit

1 stick butter or margarine	1 can peaches
½ cup brown sugar	1 can apricots
⅔ teaspoon curry powder	1 can cherries
1 can pineapple	1 can plums
1 can pears	

Drain fruit, place in baking dish. Melt butter and add curry powder and sugar. Pour over fruit and bake 1 hour at 300 degrees. Refrigerate over night, then reheat for serving. Serves 6.

Nanci Simmons

Potato Casserole

6 medium potatoes
3 tablespoons butter or margarine
2 tablespoons flour
3 cups milk
1 teaspoon salt
¼ teaspoon pepper
2 tablespoons chopped onion
Grated sharp cheddar cheese

Make white sauce by melting the margarine in saucepan or double boiler; add the flour and blend together. Slowly add the milk, stirring constantly. Add salt and pepper. Stir until thickened. Pare potatoes and slice thin. Place half the potatoes in greased 2-quart casserole; cover with half the sauce and onion.

Add remaining potatoes and onion, then the remaining sauce. Cover and bake in 350-degree oven about 1 hour. Sprinkle grated sharp cheddar cheese over top and cook in oven till bubbly. Note: cream of mushroom soup or cream of celery soup may be substituted for the white sauce.

Nanci Simmons

Vegetable Medley

2 packages frozen lima beans, cook and drain
2 packages frozen green peas, cook and drain
1 (No. 2) can French green beans, heat and drain
1 cup sour cream
1 cup mayonnaise
2 teaspoons mustard
1 teaspoon Worcestershire sauce
Dash Tabasco
1 tablespoon grated onion
½ cup cooking oil
4 hard-cooked eggs, cut up

Mix together last 8 ingredients. Pour over hot vegetables and mix well. Also very good served cold. This dish goes very well with turkey or ham.

Lealice Dehoney

Broccoli and Rice Casserole

1 stick margarine
1 small onion, chopped
1 package chopped broccoli
1 small jar Cheez Whiz
2 cups cooked rice, lightly salted

Sauté chopped onion in margarine. Cook broccoli in lightly salted water until just crisp tender. Put two cups lightly salted cooked rice in buttered baking dish. Add broccoli, onion, and Cheez Whiz. Bake in 350-degree oven until bubbly. Note: This is a good recipe to double.

Anna Lou Cummings
Nanci Simmons

Consommé Rice

1 can beef consommé	1 beef bouillon cube
1 can water	1 teaspoon salt
1 stick margarine	1½ cups rice

Heat first 5 ingredients. Add rice, pour into greased casserole, and bake at 350 degrees for 40 minutes.

Anne King

Rice and Water Chestnuts

1 stick margarine
1 cup uncooked rice
1 can condensed onion soup
1 can water
1 can thinly sliced water chestnuts, drained
1 can mushrooms (optional)
1 cup pecan halves

Melt margarine. Add rice, onion soup, and water. Simmer for about a minute. Add water chestnuts and mushrooms. Pour into a greased 8-by-11-inch glass baking dish. Bake at 350 degrees for 45 minutes to 1 hour. Top with pecan halves the last 15 minutes of baking. Watch this casserole carefully because it is easy to overcook. If mixture is hot when you put it in the oven, it will not take it as long to bake.

Clarisse Durrette

Marinated Green Beans

1½ cups vinegar
⅔ cup water
2 cups sugar
3 tablespoons salad oil
3 cans green beans or enough fresh cooked green beans
    for 6 servings
3 large onions, thinly sliced

In saucepan combine vinegar, water, sugar, and salad oil. Bring to a boil and pour over beans and onions in a casserole. Let it stand for at least 2 hours. Then pour off liquid and serve.

Frances Moore

International Recipes

Teriyaki Steak

3 pounds flank steak or tenderloin of beef
½ cup salad oil
4 tablespoons sesame seeds
½ cup soy sauce
3 cloves fresh garlic
¼ cup sugar
1 small piece fresh ginger root (or ¼ teaspoon ground ginger)

Brown sesame seeds in oil and cool. Put sesame seeds and oil in blender. Add to blender the soy sauce, garlic, sugar, and ginger root. Blend together and pour over meat. Marinate at least 3 hours. Grill meat over charcoal or oven broil approximately 5 minutes on each side and serve hot. Heat marinade sauce to boiling. Boil 2 minutes. Serve sauce and steamed rice with meat.

Mrs. Henry Holley

Green Bean and Asparagus Casserole

1 (16 ounce) can green beans
1 (15- to 16-ounce) can green asparagus
1 small can water chestnuts
1 small can mushrooms
1 (10-ounce) can cream of mushroom soup
½ teaspoon salt
½ teaspoon garlic powder
1 can French fried onion rings

Mix all ingredients except onion rings and pour into casserole dish. Top with onion rings. Bake at 350 degrees for 20 minutes or until onion rings are golden brown and mixture is bubbly.

Mrs. Henry Holley

Fresh Fruit Salad

2½ to 3 cups mixed fresh fruit   **2 tablespoons honey**
½ cup sour cream

Mix ingredients together and chill.

Mrs. Henry Holley

Viennese Sachertorte

1 cup shortening	**1 cup sugar**
8 eggs, separated	**1 cup self-rising flour**
1 (12-ounce) package chocolate chips, melted	**Apricot preserves**

Icing: (This is double the amount of icing needed for this recipe.)

⅛ cup water	**1 cup sugar**
1 (12-ounce) chocolate chips	**2 tablespoons butter**
	Whipped cream

Cream shortening and sugar. Add one egg yolk at a time, beating well after each addition. Add melted chocolate and flour; beat well. Beat egg whites until stiff and fold into above mixture carefully. Pour into a 10-inch springform pan. Bake at 350 degrees for 45 minutes. Cool. When cool, cut in half horizontally and spread apricot preserves between layers. Icing: In top of double boiler put water and second package of chocolate chips; stir until chocolate has melted. Beat until smooth with hand mixer. Gradually add sugar and butter and beat until smooth. Ice torte. When icing is dry and set, wrap torte with plastic wrap and freeze overnight. When ready to serve, carefully remove plastic wrap immediately or it will stick. Serve with whipped cream. One sachertorte makes 30 servings. Note: Sachertorte can be made up to a month ahead of time.

Bertha Berg
Mrs. Walter H. Bunzl

Mrs. Bunzl's Duck Recipe

2 to 3 ducks (allow ¼ duck per serving)
1 (8-ounce) bottle chili sauce
1 cup brown sugar
Juice of 2 (16-ounce) cans Bing cherries
1 large can frozen orange juice
Orange slices

Cook duck on rack to remove grease. Cool. When cool, quarter ducks and refrigerate. Combine remaining ingredients and heat to boiling. Put sauce in heavy pot and add quartered ducks. Bake in 350-degree oven for 1 hour, basting frequently. Serve on hot platter with Bing cherries and orange slices. Very elegant and delicious!

Mrs. Bunzl's Lentil Soup

1 (16-ounce) package lentils
2 bouillon cubes
2 tablespoons soup greens (instant dehydrated)
1 to 2 potatoes, peeled and cubed
Kosher weiners, sliced thin (about 1 weiner per serving)

Use the basic recipe on the package of lentils and add remaining ingredients. Put white vinegar on the table for guests to add to soup as they wish. Mrs. Bunzl says this is so satisfying that you need no accompaniment. However, if you choose to serve bread, use either pumpernickel or rye.

Mrs. Bunzl's Goulash

2 pounds of beef or veal	Cayenne pepper to taste
Cooking oil	1 (12-ounce) can tomato paste
3 large onions, sliced thin	Sour cream (optional)
¼ cup butter	Potatoes or noodles

Cut meat in cubes and brown in a small amount of oil. Remove meat from pan and discard grease. Sauté onions in butter; remove from pan. Place meat, onions, cayenne pepper, and tomato paste in large pot. Cover pot and cook 2 hours. Add heated sour cream just before serving, if desired. Serve with potatoes or noodles.

Bulgogi (Korean Barbecued Beef)

2 to 3 pounds thinly sliced beef
4 tablespoons soy sauce
1 teaspoon sugar
1 teaspoon sesame oil
2 tablespoons chopped green onions

Mix last 4 ingredients and pour over meat. Marinate meat 2 hours at room temperature. Cook meat on charcoal grill until tender. Serves 5.

Dr. Rosaio An

Japchae

2 carrots, cut in half lengthwise and thinly sliced
1 bundle watercress
7 ounces transparent noodles, soaked in warm water 30 minutes
Dried mushrooms, soaked in warm water 30 minutes
1 large onion, thinly sliced
¼ pound beef, chopped in small pieces
1 teaspoon sesame oil
1 teaspoon soy sauce
Dash monosodium glutamate (MSG)

Steam all ingredients except beef, sesame oil, soy sauce, and MSG. Cook them lightly. Brown chopped beef with a few dashes of salt and cook until tender. Place all ingredients in saucepan over warm heat and add MSG, sesame oil, and soy sauce. Serves 5.

Dr. Rosaio An

Red Snapper with Mushrooms

1 red snapper, average size   1 tablespoon vinegar
1 (3-ounce) can mushrooms   1 teaspoon salt

Soak fish with vinegar and salt 10 minutes. Bake at 350 degrees for 40 minutes or until done. Brown fish on broil for a few minutes toward the end of the baking time. Drain mushrooms and brown in buttered pan. Pour mushrooms over fish when serving.

Dr. Rosaio An

Cucumber Salad

2 cucumbers
1 teaspoon salt
½ teaspoon sesame seeds, baked and ground
1 teaspoon vinegar
½ teaspoon sugar

Slice cucumbers very thin. Marinate in salt for 30 minutes. Squeeze water out of cucumbers and add sesame seeds, vinegar, and sugar. Mix thoroughly and serve. Serves 5.

Dr. Rosaio An

Mandu

10 sheets egg-roll skin
2 cups cooked cabbage or cooked bean sprouts, chopped
1 cup bean cake, chopped
⅓ cup green onion, chopped
½ pound ground pork
½ pound ground beef
Cooking oil
Egg yolk

Cook ground beef, ground pork, and green onion in pan with small amount of oil until done. Add chopped bean cake toward the end of cooking. Mix these ingredients with the cabbage or bean sprouts. Cut each egg-roll skin into 4 squares. Fill each square with the mixture and fold square into a triangular form. Paste edges with egg yolk. Either steam triangles for 10 minutes or cook in a generously greased pan for 10 to 15 minutes.

Dr. Rosaio An

Roast Pork

1 pork roast	2 teaspoons cumin
1 clove garlic	½ teaspoon paprika
¾ cup lime juice	2 tablespoons salt
1 tablespoon oregano	1 pound onions

Clean the pork well by taking some of the fat from it. With a sharp pointed knife make holes in it so seasoning will sink in. Chop the garlic, add the salt, oregano, cumin, paprika, and lime juice. Soak the pork well with this seasoning mix. Slice the onions and place them on top of the pork. Leave it in refrigerator for at least 12 hours. Bake at 325 degrees for about 4 hours. Serves 8 to 10.

Mrs. Rafael Reyes

Black Beans

1 pound black beans
10 cups water
⅔ cup olive oil
4 cloves garlic
1 large onion, chopped
2 large green peppers, chopped
4 teaspoons salt
½ teaspoon paprika
¼ teaspoon oregano
1 bay leaf
2 tablespoons sugar
2 tablespoons vinegar
2 tablespoons cooking wine
2 tablespoons olive oil

Clean the beans and let them soak in water with half the green pepper. When they start peeling, cook them for approximately 45 minutes until they are soft. In a frying pan with the ⅔ cup of olive oil, fry the chopped onion and garlic and later add the remaining green peppers. Put approximately one cup of beans in the pan and press them to make a paste. Combine this seasoning with the rest of the beans. Add the salt, paprika, oregano, bay leaf, and sugar. Simmer covered for about 1 hour more. Add the vinegar and cooking wine and cook on low heat for about 1 hour more until they are pasty. If the beans are too watery, uncover them and cook until they become pasty. When ready to serve, add 2 tablespoons of olive oil. Serves about 8.

Mrs. Rafael Reyes

Avocado Salad

2 avocados
Vinegar
1 medium onion

Salt
Olive oil

Slice the avocado and add salt, olive oil, and vinegar. Slice onion and place on top of the avocado slices.

Mrs. Rafael Reyes

Fried Green Plantains

Plantains are Spanish bananas—big green bananas. They can be found at some large supermarkets or an international market place. Ask at your favorite grocery store.

Peel the plantains and cut them in pieces of approximately 1 inch. Fry them in cooking oil at 365 degrees for about 5 minutes. Place them on a towel to soak up the grease. Press them flat and refry at 385 degrees for about 3 minutes. Place on a towel again and salt them.

Mrs. Rafael Reyes

Fried Rice

½ cup small shrimp, canned or fresh
½ cup roast pork or ham, diced
2 eggs, beaten
2 tablespoons green peas
1 tablespoon chopped green onion
4 cups cooked rice
2 teaspoons salt
8 tablespoons peanut oil
1 tablespoon raisins (optional)

Soak raisins for about 10 minutes. Heat 2 tablespoons of oil in pan. Pour in the beaten egg and stir-fry quickly until the eggs are in tiny pieces. Remove from pan. Heat another 3 tablespoons of oil, stir-fry shrimp and pork, add soaked raisins and green peas, fry about 1 minute, and remove from pan. Heat another 3 teaspoons of oil in same frying pan, fry the onion and cooked rice, mixing well. Add salt. Reduce heat and stir until rice is thoroughly heated, then add all other ingredients. Combine well and serve on pretty platter.

Mrs. Stephen S. F. Chen

Oil Dripped Chicken

1 (2-pound) young chicken or fryer
2 green onions
3 slices ginger
1 star anise
5 tablespoons soy sauce
1 tablespoon white vinegar
1 tablespoon shredded green onion
1 teaspoon brown peppercorn powder
2 tablespoons sesame oil
5 cups peanut oil
Sliced orange wedges
Pimento slices
Olives
Parsley

Wash chicken and dry with paper towels. Cut the chicken down the back but do not cut all the way through. This is so you can marinate it for at least 1 hour. Combine the soy sauce, wine, 2 green onions, ginger slices, and star anise and pour over the chicken in the pan. Leave to marinate.

In a steamer or large pot, steam the chicken with the marinade for 20 minutes or until it feels tender with a fork.

Heat the 5 cups of peanut oil in a deep fryer or heavy frying pan. Remove the steamed chicken (reserve the marinade) and very carefully place it in the deep hot oil. Fry it for about 3 minutes until the skin is crispy and brown. Remove the chicken and allow to cool briefly.

If you have the proper utensils, you will be able to learn to prepare the rest of this recipe in true Chinese fashion.

Place the chicken opened out on a cutting board. Using a *very* sharp cleaver, cut the chicken body in rectangular pieces (bone and all). The drumsticks should be cut in slices across the bone, the wings cut at the joints. Now slip a very wide knife or spatula under the chicken and remove to serving platter. Arrange in mound to resemble a chicken shape. Place drumsticks on each side and wings across the top.

Sprinkle shredded green onion and peppercorn powder on chicken. Then pour heated sesame oil and 2 tablespoons of the reserved marinade over the chicken and serve.

Author's note: For those of us not skilled in Chinese cooking, this recipe sounds ridiculous. I could never make it look anything like a chicken, but I have seen the finished product and it makes a great buffet display, and it is delicious. In order to get the flavor, cook the chicken as directed. When you remove it from the fryer, place it on a cutting board to cool. Using your sharpest knife, cut the chicken off the bones and place on serving platter in an attractive way (a mound or a ring). Finish the garnish as directed. Add thin sliced orange wedges, pimento slices, olives, and parsley.

Mrs. Stephen S. F. Chen

Shrimp with Cashew Nuts

⅔ pound small fresh shrimp
4 ounces cashew nuts
10 green onions, cut in 1-inch pieces
10 slices ginger
3 cups peanut oil
½ egg white
1 tablespoon cornstarch
½ teaspoon salt
1 tablespoon wine
¼ teaspoon salt
1 teaspoon sesame oil

Clean and peel shrimp and pat dry, then mix with egg white, cornstarch, and ½ teaspoon salt and soak for at least an hour. Fry the cashew nuts in heated oil over low heat until brown (about 3 minutes). Remove, drain, and set aside to cool. Heat the same oil again (about 350 degrees), pour in shrimp, and fry for half a minute. Remove shrimp and drain oil from pan. With another 2 tablespoons of oil fry the green onion and ginger slices, add shrimp, wine, ¼ teaspoon salt, and sesame oil quickly, then stir until thoroughly mixed over high heat. Turn off heat, add the cashew nuts, and serve.

Mrs. Stephen S. F. Chen

Sweet and Sour Pork

1 pound pork tenderloin
2 green peppers
4 slices pineapple, or 1 cup Cantonese pickles
3 tablespoons vinegar
4 tablespoons sugar
4 tablespoons tomato catsup
4 tablespoons cold water
½ teaspoon salt
½ tablespoon soy sauce
1 tablespoon cornstarch
1 tablespoon cold water
1 egg yolk
6 cups peanut oil
3 teaspoons cornstarch
1 teaspoon salt
1 teaspoon sesame oil
½ cup cornstarch

Pound pork with the back of a cleaver to tenderize, then cut into 1-inch cubes. Combine ½ teaspoon salt, soy sauce, 1 table-spoon cornstarch, and 1 tablespoon water to make marinade. Soak pork in marinade for at least ½ hour. Cut green pepper into halves, remove seeds and membranes, and cut into squares. Set aside. Heat peanut oil. While oil is heating, dip each piece of pork in egg yolk and coat with the ½ cup of cornstarch. When oil is ready, fry pork until brown and done (about 2 minutes); remove from oil. Reheat oil and fry pork once more until crispy. Remove pork and drain off oil from frying pan, reserving 2 tablespoons. Put back into the frying pan the 2 tablespoons of oil. Add green pepper and pineapple and fry, stirring constantly. Remove pan from heat. Combine vinegar, sugar, catsup, the 4 tablespoons cold water, 3 teaspoons cornstarch, 1 teaspoon salt, and the sesame oil to make the seasoning sauce. Add seasoning sauce to frying pan and continue to stir-fry until thickened. Turn off heat. Add pork and mix well. Serve immediately.

Mrs. Stephen S. F. Chen

Egg Rolls

6 ounces lean pork (or ham or roast pork)
4 ounces shrimp, shredded
½ pound cabbage, shredded in strips about 1½ inches long
6 ounces bean sprouts
2 ounces spring onions, shredded
20 pieces egg-roll skins
½ tablespoon soy sauce
1 teaspoon cornstarch
¼ teaspoon salt
1 teaspoon cornstarch
1 tablespoon soy sauce
1 teaspoon salt
6 cups peanut oil
½ cup cold water
1 tablespoon cornstarch
1 tablespoon cold water
1 tablespoon flour

Cut pork into string shapes. Combine the ½ tablespoon soy sauce and the first teaspoon of cornstarch and marinate pork in this mixture. Combine the ¼ teaspoon salt and the remaining teaspoon cornstarch and marinate shrimp in this mixture. Heat 5 tablespoons of oil in frying pan and stir-fry pork about ½ minute. Drain and set aside. Use same oil to stir-fry shrimp until done. Remove shrimp from oil and put with pork. Add cabbage to frying pan; stir-fry a moment and then add the 1 tablespoon soy sauce, the 1 teaspoon salt, and the ½ cup cold water. Cover with lid and cook 2 minutes. Then add pork and shrimp. Add bean sprouts and onions and stir-fry another ½ minute over high heat. Make a paste using the remaining 1 tablespoon cornstarch and 1 tablespoon cold water. Stir paste into mixture in frying pan and continue stirring until thickened. Remove from heat and put into mixing bowl. Place 2 tablespoons filling on each egg-roll skin, about 1 inch from the edge that is toward you. Roll once or twice, then fold right side toward center, then left side toward center, and continue rolling into a tight roll. Make flour paste using remaining 1 tablespoon of flour and add 1½ teaspoons of water. Stick outer edge of egg-roll skin to roll with flour paste. Place this side face down to hold tightly and to keep its shape until time for frying. Heat the 6 cups peanut oil in deep pan and deep fry egg rolls 10 at a time for about 3 minutes or until golden. Serve with soy sauce and brown vinegar.

Mrs. Stephen S. F. Chen

Almond Jelly Chinese Style

⅓ ounce agar-agar, or 1 envelope gelatin
5 cups cold water
2 tablespoons sugar
3 tablespoons evaporated milk
4 tablespoons almond syrup or 2 teaspoons almond extract
4 cups cold sugar water (4 cups cold water
  and 2 cups sugar)
1 cup diced fresh fruit (assorted) or canned fruit cocktail

After cleaning the agar-agar with water, squeeze and place in a deep pan; cook with 5 cups of cold water for 15 minutes over medium heat. If using gelatin, dissolve the powder in 4 tablespoons water. Add 2 tablespoons sugar to agar-agar or gelatin. When the sugar is blended, strain into a big bowl. Add milk and 2 tablespoons almond syrup (or 1 teaspoon almond extract). Stir briskly until thoroughly mixed. Let cool and remove to refrigerator for at least 2 hours or until firm. Remove the chilled almond jelly from refrigerator and cut into small pieces, then place in a soup bowl or individual dessert bowls. Place the diced fruit on top of the almond jelly, pour in the cold sugar water and splash the remaining almond syrup or almond extract. Serve.

Mrs. Stephen S. F. Chen

Mexican Fiesta

2 large bags Fritos, crushed
Meat sauce with red beans
3 cups cooked rice
6 or 8 quartered tomatoes
1 or 2 diced onions
1 (6-ounce) jar sliced olives
1 large lettuce, shredded
Shredded sharp cheddar cheese (allow ¼ cup per serving)
Bottled hot sauce

Meat sauce:

1 pound ground beef
1½ cups chopped onion
¾ cup chopped green pepper
3 cloves garlic, chopped
3 (8-ounce) cans seasoned tomato sauce
1 (6-ounce) can tomato paste
⅓ cup water
2 teaspoons Worcestershire sauce
1½ teaspoons salt
½ teaspoon pepper
1 (8-ounce) can red kidney beans, drained

Brown meat and drain off excess fat. Add onion, garlic, and green pepper and cook about 2 minutes. Add tomato paste, water, Worcestershire sauce, salt, pepper, and drained kidney beans. Cover and simmer 2 hours.

Place Fritos on plate, then rice, then meat sauce. Cover with your choice of remaining ingredients and eat. Serves 8.

Lealice Dehoney

Breads

Mixes

With a supply of ready mixes on hand you can add a delicious touch of elegance to the most simple meal. Hot breads will make you famous, and you can make them with ease. Use your imagination for variations when making biscuits or muffins: add ¼ to ½ cup shredded cheese to mixture, a teaspoon of jelly or jam in the center of a muffin, or ½ cup blueberries. Add ½ teaspoon onion flakes to the cornbread mix to accompany a seafood dinner.

Homemade mixes are much cheaper than packaged mixes. One morning spent in the kitchen preparing the mixes saves on the food budget and assures you of always having a quick, delicious hot bread on short notice. Your family and guests will love you!

Biscuit Mix

8 cups flour
1⅓ cups nonfat dry milk
5 tablespoons baking powder
1 tablespoon salt
1 cup solid shortening (butter, margarine, or vegetable shortening)

Combine all ingredients (except shortening), mixing thoroughly with a fork. Work in shortening with fingertips until very fine. Store in a tight container in a cool, dry place. Note: If self-rising flour is used, omit salt and baking powder.

Mrs. E. Clarence Shealy

Biscuits

2⅔ cups Biscuit Mix   ¾ cup cold water

In mixing bowl, stir water into Biscuit Mix with a fork. Turn out on lightly floured board and knead lightly. Pat to about ½ inch thickness and cut with floured cutter, or pinch off pieces and roll in hands to form biscuits, whichever is quicker for you. Bake at 425 degrees for 10 to 12 minutes. Yields 18 biscuits. Note: My family prefers a little sugar added to the mix—about ⅓ cup to 18-biscuit recipe.

Short Cake

4 cups Biscuit Mix   **Melted margarine**
½ cup sugar   **Fresh fruit**
2 eggs, beaten   **Whipped cream or ice cream**
½ cup water

Put Mix in bowl; add sugar. Stir in beaten eggs and water mixing lightly with fork to form a soft dough. Divide dough in half. Press half of the dough into a 9-inch layer cake pan. Brush lightly with melted margarine. Spread remaining dough over first layer, leaving top layer rough. Bake at 425 degrees for 25 to 30 minutes. Separate layers and brush with melted margarine. Stack with fresh fruit. Serve warm with whipped cream or ice cream.

Cornbread Mix

4 cups flour   ⅔ cup sugar
4 cups cornmeal   ¼ cup baking powder
2 cups nonfat dry milk   1 tablespoon salt

Mix all ingredients well with a fork. Store in an airtight container in a cool, dry place.

Mrs. E. Clarence Shealy

Cornbread or Corn Muffins

2¼ cups Cornbread Mix
1 cup water
1 egg
¼ cup vegetable oil

Mix all ingredients together thoroughly. Pour batter into a well-greased 8- or 9-inch square baking pan or a 12-cup muffin pan. Bake at 400 degrees until done. Note: For a Southern-flavored corn bread or muffin, use buttermilk instead of water.

Angel Biscuits

5 cups self-rising flour
⅓ cup sugar
1 teaspoon soda
1 heaping cup vegetable shortening
2 packages active dry yeast
¼ cup lukewarm water
2 cups buttermilk

Sift flour after measuring and again with sugar and soda. This mixture should be in a large mixing bowl. Cut in shortening with a pastry blender. Dissolve the yeast in warm water. Stir the buttermilk and yeast mixture into shortening and flour mixture until thoroughly moistened. Place dough on floured board and knead a minute or two. Roll out to desired thickness and cut into rounds. Bake on ungreased cookie sheet at 400 degrees about 12 minutes or until lightly browned. Yield: about 40 biscuits.

The dough may be refrigerated in a covered bowl or plastic bag. Take out and use as needed. It is good to let the dough rise at room temperature an hour before baking, but this is not absolutely necessary. For a quick breakfast treat, roll out dough, cut into rounds, and bake. The biscuits will rise enough while baking. Also, you may cut rounds and place on cookie sheet and refrigerate until an hour before baking. This can be done the night before.

Anne King

Quick Cobbler Topping

1 stick margarine, softened to room temperature
1 cup flour
1½ teaspoons baking powder
½ teaspoon salt

Mix all ingredients together with a fork to form a stiff batter. Spoon over fruit or other ingredients and bake at 375 degrees for 35 to 40 minutes. Note: If self-rising flour is used, omit baking powder and salt.

Mrs. E. Clarence Shealy

Fruit Cobbler

For fruit cobbler, add 2 tablespoons sugar to Quick Cobbler Topping recipe, or sprinkle cobbler with sugar when done. Serve fruit cobbler hot with ice cream, whipped topping, or sprinkled with cinnamon, sugar, or nutmeg.

Meat Cobbler

For chicken or other meat, add a teaspoon of poultry seasoning to Quick Cobbler Topping recipe. For a rich-tasting, delicious chicken pie, substitute chicken fat for margarine.

Pastry Mix

6 cups flour
1 tablespoon salt
2½ cups white vegetable shortening

Mix all ingredients to coarse meal consistency. Store in a cool place or in the refrigerator. Always stir with a fork before using, as the high amount of shortening tends to settle. Makes about 8 cups. This is a good recipe to double.

Mrs. E. Clarence Shealy

Pie Crust

2 cups Pastry Mix   **¼ cup (approx.) ice water**

Stir Pastry Mix with a fork. As you stir, sprinkle ice water over the mix with the other hand. Dough should just cling together to form a ball. Handle as little as possible. Pat or roll out on a lightly floured board. Place in a pie plate. Pinch around edges to flute. Makes 2 (8-inch) crusts. Pie crusts can be baked until lightly browned, then put in a plastic bag or aluminum foil and refrigerated for several days. This cuts down on preparation and cooling time for fillings that require a prebaked, cooled crust.

Six-Week All-Bran Muffins

4 cups All-Bran	2 cups All-Bran
3 cups sugar	2 cups boiling water
5 cups flour, unsifted	1 cup vegetable shortening
5 teaspoons soda	4 eggs, beaten
2 teaspoons salt	1 quart buttermilk
2 cups raisins, optional	

In a large bowl mix together 4 cups All-Bran, sugar, flour, soda, and salt. Soak 2 cups All-Bran in the boiling water to which has been added the vegetable shortening. Add to above mixture. Then add eggs and buttermilk and stir well. Fold in raisins, if desired. Cover and refrigerate overnight. Bake as many muffins as needed at 400 degrees for 15 to 20 minutes. The batter keeps up to six weeks in the refrigerator. Note: Make these in minipans and serve with whipped cream cheese.

Janis Kelly

Six-Week Raisin Bran Muffins

1 large box raisin bran flakes	4 eggs, beaten
3 cups sugar	1 cup vegetable oil
5 cups flour	1 quart buttermilk
5 teaspoons soda	1 teaspoon cinnamon
2 teaspoons salt	

In a large bowl mix cereal, sugar, flour, soda, and salt. Add eggs, oil, and buttermilk. Mix well. Cover and store in the refrigerator. (Do not freeze.) To bake, fill greased muffin tins ⅔ full and bake at 400 degrees 10 to 12 minutes. Note: 1 large box 40% Bran Flakes may be used if desired.

Nanci Simmons
Betty Massey

No-Knead Refrigerator Rolls

2 cups warm (not hot) water	2 teaspoons salt
2 packages yeast	¼ cup shortening, softened
⅓ cup sugar	6½ to 7 cups flour
1 egg	

Put yeast, sugar, salt, and about half the flour in a bowl. Beat thoroughly about 2 minutes. Add egg and shortening; beat in and gradually add the rest of the flour until you have smooth, firm dough. Cover with a double-thickness damp cloth or a plastic bag. Place in the refrigerator. Punch down occasionally. Make into rolls 1½ to 2 hours before baking time. Note: This will keep for at least a week, permitting you to use just the amount needed each time. It must be punched down to prevent its becoming too sour.

Mrs. E. Clarence Shealy

Cloverleaf Rolls

Grease muffin tins. Pinch enough No-Knead dough to make nut-size rolls and place three of these in one tin. Fill muffin tins this way. Allow to rise several hours in a warm place and bake at 375 degrees about 15 minutes or until nicely browned.

Cinnamon Rolls

No-Knead dough	Sugar
1 stick margarine	Cinnamon

Start with ¾ cup sugar and ¼ cup cinnamon. Add each ingredient as needed for spreading consistency. Do not let it become dry. Melt margarine; add sugar and cinnamon to make very spreadable paste. Roll out half of dough to ½ inch thickness. Spread with cinnamon mixture, roll up, and cut in 1-inch slices. Place in a greased cake pan (6 to 7 rolls). Let rise for several hours. Bake at 375 degrees about 20 minutes or until nicely browned.

Loaf Bread

Place No-Knead dough in greased loaf pan. Allow to rise several hours. Bake at 375 degrees about 30 minutes until nicely browned. When done, bread sounds hollow when tapped on top.

Banana Nut Bread

¼ cup shortening	1½ cups flour, sifted
½ cup sugar	2 teaspoons baking powder
1 egg, well beaten	½ teaspoon salt
1 cup bran	½ teaspoon soda
2 tablespoons water	1 teaspoon vanilla
1½ cups mashed bananas	½ cup chopped nuts

Cream shortening and sugar. Add egg, vanilla, and water. Stir in mashed bananas. Sift together dry ingredients and add to above mixture. Stir in nuts. Pour batter into greased loaf pan and bake at 350 degrees for 1 hour.

Lealice Dehoney

Pancakes

1½ cups sifted all-purpose flour
1 teaspoon salt
3 tablespoons sugar
1¾ teaspoons double-acting baking powder
2 eggs, separated
3 tablespoons melted butter or vegetable oil
1 to 1¼ cups milk

Add the two egg yolks to 1 cup of milk. Mix all ingredients together (except egg whites) and blend well. Beat egg whites until stiff but not dry, and then fold them into the batter. If the batter is too stiff, add the ¼ cup of milk. Grease skillet lightly and preheat. Test by letting a drop or two of water fall on it. If it spatters, it is ready to use. Pour the batter carefully from a large spoon. When the cakes begin to bubble on top, lift and turn with a spatula. Turn only once. The second side takes about half as long to cook as the first side. Makes 12 to 14 4-inch pancakes.

Easy Rolls

1 package yeast	2½ cups Bisquick
¾ cup warm water	

Dissolve yeast in warm water. Add Bisquick. Beat until smooth. Knead on a floured board. Put dough back into bowl and let rest 10 minutes. Roll into desired shapes and let rise 1 to 2 hours or until doubled in bulk. Bake at 400 degrees on a lightly greased pan until done. Note: Brush melted butter on top of rolls either before or immediately after baking.

Lealice Dehoney

Hot Cheese Loaf

1 pound sharp cheddar cheese (grated)
1 heaping cup cracker crumbs (rolled fine)
1 medium-size jar chopped pimento
3 eggs
¾ cup sugar
1 scant tablespoon salt
½ cup vinegar
1 cup milk
1 tablespoon butter

Beat eggs well; add sugar and salt. Stir in vinegar, milk, and butter. Mix well. Cook over medium heat, stirring constantly until thickened and bubbly. Remove from heat; add cheese, crackers, and pimento. Spoon into well-greased mold. Bake at 375 degrees for 30 minutes. Remove by running knife around mold.

From Pat Cole's file via Jewel Nelson

Cliff Barrow's Rolls

1 cup self-rising flour   1 cup vanilla ice cream

Mix together until smooth. Fill greased muffin tins one-half full. Bake at 400 degrees for 10 minutes. Makes 12 rolls.

Crepes

Basic Crepe Batter

¾ cup all-purpose flour
Pinch of salt
1¼ cups milk

1 egg yolk
1 egg
1 tablespoon light oil

Sift flour into mixing bowl. Add salt, egg yolk, whole egg, and half the milk. Stir with wire whisk until smooth. Add remainder of milk and oil. Place in blender and blend for 10 seconds. Cook as detailed on p. 53. Crepe pancakes may be made ahead of time, stacked, and kept in the refrigerator for up to 2 weeks. This recipe makes 12 crepes.

When filling crepes, be sure filling is firm enough to hold its shape when the crepe is rolled.

Betty Van Gerpen

Basic White Sauce for Crepes

6 tablespoons butter
6 tablespoons flour
½ teaspoon salt

¼ teaspoon white pepper
2 cups half-and-half
4 egg yolks

Scald half-and-half. Melt the butter in saucepan over low heat or in double boiler. Add flour, stirring constantly until mixture thickens. Then season. Pour a few spoonfuls of white sauce over the beaten egg yolks. Stir this into the remaining sauce and cook slowly, stirring constantly until thick.

Betty Van Gerpen

Spinach Crepes
(Crepes à la Florentine)

2 pounds chopped frozen spinach
4 tablespoons butter
3 teaspoons grated onion
4 tablespoons bread crumbs
1 teaspoon salt
¼ teaspoon pepper
Dash nutmeg
2 cups White Sauce

Cook spinach according to package directions until tender. Drain. Heat butter in skillet; add onion, bread crumbs, and the seasonings. Set aside. When cooled, fold in spinach and White Sauce.

Betty Van Gerpen

Mushroon Crepes with Ham

8 crepes
3 tablespoons butter
½ onion finely chopped
1½ cups mushrooms (thinly sliced)
2 tablespoons lemon juice
½ cup chicken broth
8 thin slices boiled ham
½ cup grated Gruyère cheese
¼ cup whipping cream
1 tablespoon cornstarch dissolved in 2 tablespoons cold water
Salt and pepper

Sauté the onion in the butter until soft. Add the thinly sliced mushroomms. Cook for 1 minute. Add chicken broth and cook over high heat for 1 minute. Lower heat and *gradually* add grated cheese and cream. Add cornstarch dissolved in water. Add salt and pepper to taste. Lay a piece of boiled ham on each crepe. Put 2 tablespoons of mushroom mixture over the ham and roll the crepe. Place in preheated 400-degree over for 15 minutes. Serve immediately.

Betty Van Gerpen

Crepes Fruit De Mer

8 crepes
2 ounces sherry
Salt, pepper, and paprika
1 pound scallops (boiled)
2 pounds shrimp (boiled and peeled)
White Sauce

Add sherry, salt, pepper, and dash of paprika to White Sauce. Fold in scallops and shrimp. Place 2 tablespoons mixture on each crepe. Fold, place in buttered dish, folds down. Bake at 400 degrees for 15 minutes. Serve immediately.

Betty Van Gerpen

Chicken Crepes

8 crepes
3 pounds cooked diced chicken
2 ounces white wine
White Sauce
Salt and pepper

Add white wine to White Sauce. Gently fold in diced chicken. Place 2 tablespoons mixture on crepe. Roll. Place seam side down in buttered dish. Bake 15 minutes in 400-degree oven.

Learn to use leftover chicken or turkey for crepes. Mix with mushrooms, pimento, and Basic White Sauce and have elegant leftover dinners! Also use ham with asparagus, and don't forget crab, tuna, or salmon with sauce. Use your imagination and have fun with crepes!

Betty Van Gerpen

Strawberry Crepes à la Perigourdene

3 cups fresh strawberries (sliced and sprinkled with powdered sugar)
1 large box vanilla instant pudding
1 pint whipped topping
Toasted almonds (slivered)

Prepare pudding according to directions on package. When almost set, fold in half of whipped topping. Place 1 tablespoon pudding mixture on crepe, then 2 teaspoons strawberries. Roll crepe. Place on plate seam side down. Put a dot of whipped topping and garnish with slivered almonds.

These should be made at the last minute, so why not prepare them at the table? This can easily be done, and your guests will think you are marvelous! If crepes are made at the table, make sure the crepes are on an attractive tray; the pudding, strawberries, and cream in nice silver, china, or crystal dishes. Your guests will love you for all the effort!

Betty Van Gerpen

Toffee Crepes

8 Heath Bars   **1 pint whipped topping**
4 tablespoons butter

Crush 8 Heath Bars finely. Combine with 4 tablespoons soft butter and 1 pint whipped topping. Blend gently but thoroughly. Place 2 tablespoons mixture on each crepe. Roll. Place on plate, seam side down.

Betty Van Gerpen

Garnishes for Crepes

Always be conscious of how crepes look on the serving tray or dish. Each serving dish should have a special garnish. Plan ahead. Decide early in the week what will make your crepes especially attractive.

Have on hand: Parsley and watercress (fresh and washed ahead), fresh mushrooms (sautéed gently in butter early in the day), red caviar (looks great sprinkled over White Sauce), paprika, toasted almonds, chives, thin lemon slices (great with seafood crepes).

Be creative; decide what looks best for each dish. You are building a reputation, so don't let up now. People never forget attractive surroundings, food, flowers, and good company.

Desserts

Applesauce Cake

1 cup margarine	1 tablespoon soda
2 cups sugar	1 tablespoon cinnamon
2 eggs	1 teaspoon cloves
2½ cups applesauce	1 teaspoon nutmeg
2 teaspoons corn syrup	½ cup raisins
3 cups flour	1 cup chopped nuts
½ teaspoon salt	

Cream 1 cup margarine with 2 cups sugar. Add eggs, 1 at a time. Combine applesauce and corn syrup. Sift dry ingredients together. Add dry ingredients and applesauce mixture alternately to butter-sugar mixture. Fold in raisins and chopped nuts. Pour batter into greased tube pan and bake at 325 degrees 1½ hours. Leave in pan until cool.

Frosting:

½ cup margarine	¼ cup milk
1 cup brown sugar	2 cups confectioners' sugar

Melt margarine; add brown sugar and boil over low heat, stirring constantly for 2 minutes. Add milk; stir until mixture comes to a boil. Remove from heat and cool. Slowly add confectioners' sugar. Beat until thick enough to spread.

Ginny Osburn

Baked Devil's Float

1 cup flour	2 teaspoons baking powder
1 tablespoon cocoa	2 tablespoons melted butter
¾ cup sugar	½ teaspoon vanilla
¼ teaspoon salt	½ cup chopped nuts
½ cup milk	

Sift flour, cocoa, sugar, salt, and baking powder together. Mix milk, melted butter, vanilla, and nuts, and combine. Pour into well-buttered baking dish and *spoon* hot sauce (see below) over it. Bake at 350 degrees about 40 minutes. Serve with ice cream or whipped cream on top. Serves 8.

Sauce:

½ cup white sugar	½ cup brown sugar
1 tablespoon cocoa	1 cup hot water

Mix all ingredients until well blended.

Frances Moore

Caramel Cake

1 package yellow cake mix
1 small package instant vanilla pudding
½ cup oil
¾ cup water
4 eggs
1 teaspoon vanilla

Put ingredients in mixer and beat until well mixed. Bake in 2 cookie sheet pans (with sides) which have been greased and lined with wax paper. Bake at 350 degrees for 15 minutes. Cut each cake in half to make 4 layers.

Caramel Icing:

2 packages light brown sugar	1½ teaspoons vanilla
2 small cans evaporated milk	Pinch baking powder
2 sticks margarine	

Melt margarine and add milk and sugar. Mix well. Cook over low-to-medium heat, stirring occasionally until mixture forms a soft ball when dropped in cool water. Let icing cook to lukewarm and add vanilla and baking powder. Beat slightly and ice cake.

Barbara Nunnally

Cheese Cake

2⅔ cups graham cracker crumbs
3 tablespoons confectioners' sugar
1 stick margarine, melted
1¼ cups sugar
1 teaspoon vanilla
1 cup hot water
1 large package cream cheese, room temperature
1 package lemon gelatin
1 large can evaporated milk, chilled

Combine graham cracker crumbs, confectioners' sugar, and melted margarine. Set a small amount of mixture aside to sprinkle on top of cheese cake. Press remaining mixture into a 9½-by-13-inch pan. Dissolve gelatin in hot water and set aside. Beat sugar and vanilla into cheese. Whip milk until stiff. Combine all ingredients and whip until mixed thoroughly. Pour into crumb crust and sprinkle reserved crumb mixture on top. Cover and place in freezer overnight.

Lealice Dehoney

Chocolate Cake (Waldorf Astoria)

½ cup butter or margarine
2 cups sugar
4 squares bitter chocolate, melted
2 eggs
2 cups cake flour
1 teaspoon salt
2 teaspoons baking powder
2 teaspoons vanilla
1½ cups milk
1 cup nuts

Cream butter and sugar. Sift dry ingredients. Add melted chocolate and eggs to creamed butter and sugar mixture. Add vanilla to milk. Add sifted ingredients and milk to creamed mixture beginning and ending with dry ingredients. Fold in nuts. Pour batter into 2 greased and floured 9-inch round cake pans. Bake at 350 degrees about 35 minutes or until cake tests done.

Icing:

1 pound confectioners' sugar
1 stick butter or margarine
2 squares bitter chocolate, melted
1 teaspoon lemon juice
1 egg, beaten
1 teaspoon vanilla
1 cup chopped nuts

Combine all ingredients and beat until of spreading consistency.

Lealice Dehoney

Christmas Cake Supreme

3 cups sugar	½ pint sour cream
1 cup shortening	1 teaspoon almond extract
6 eggs separated	1 teaspoon lemon extract
¼ teaspoon soda	1 teaspoon butter flavoring
½ teaspoon salt	3 cups flour

Cream sugar and shortening and add egg yolks 1 at a time. Add the sour cream and flavoring. Add flour, soda, and salt, beating well. Fold in stiffly beaten egg whites. Pour into greased and floured tube pan. Bake at 300 degrees for 1 hour 30 minutes. Cool in pan for 5 minutes before removing.

Carolyn Self

Cola Cake

1 cup cola	½ cup buttermilk
2 sticks margarine	2 cups unsifted flour
3 tablespoons cocoa	1½ cups miniature marshmallows
2 cups sugar	2 eggs
1 teaspoon soda	1 teaspoon salt

Combine flour, sugar, cocoa, soda, and salt. Bring cola to boil and add to dry ingredients. Add melted margarine, buttermilk, eggs, and marshmallows. Bake at 350 degrees 35 to 45 minutes. Frost *while hot* with Cola Frosting.

Cola Frosting:

1 stick margarine	2 tablespoons cocoa
6 tablespoons cola	1 box confectioners' sugar
1 teaspoon vanilla	1 cup chopped pecans

Combine cola, melted margarine, and cocoa and bring to boil. Pour over sugar and add vanilla and nuts. Pour on hot cake and spread.

Anne King

Fresh Apple Cake

2 eggs	½ teaspoon salt
1¼ cups cooking oil	½ teaspoon cinnamon
2 cups sugar	½ teaspoon nutmeg
2 teaspoons vanilla	3 cups chopped apples
3 cups cake flour	1 cup chopped nuts
1½ teaspoons soda	

Beat together eggs, cooking oil, sugar, and vanilla. Sift dry ingredients. Add dry ingredients to egg mixture and beat well. Add chopped apples and nuts. Pour batter into a greased tube pan and bake at 350 degrees for 1 hour and 15 minutes. Good for coffees.

Mrs. Rudolph Davis

Fruit Cake
(5 pounds)

1 pound each dates, candied cherries , and candied pineapple
2 pounds pecans
2 cups flour (all-purpose)
2 teaspoons baking powder
½ teaspoon salt
6 medium eggs
1 cup sugar
1 tablespoon vanilla extract

Cut dates, cherries, pineapple, and nuts into mixture of flour, baking powder, and salt that has been sifted together. Beat eggs well, add sugar and vanilla extract. Pour over dredged fruit and nuts and mix well. Batter will be very thick. Pour into tube pan well greased (paper-lined bottom) and bake at 275 degrees for about 2 hours. Bake cookies bonbon size at 350 degrees approximately 25 minutes.

Ella Moore

Italian Cream Cake

1 stick margarine	1 cup buttermilk
½ cup vegetable shortening	1 teaspoon vanilla
2 cups sugar	1 cup pecans, chopped
5 egg yolks	1 can coconut
2 cups + 2 tablespoons flour	5 egg whites, stiffly beaten
1 teaspoon soda	

Cream sugar, shortening, and margarine. Beat until smooth. Add egg yolks and blend well. Combine flour and soda and sift three times. Add flour mixture alternately with buttermilk. Add vanilla, coconut, and nuts and then fold in egg whites. Pour into 3 greased and floured 8-inch round pans. Bake at 350 degrees for 25 minutes.

Frosting:

1 (8-ounce) package cream cheese
¾ stick margarine
1 box confectioners' sugar
1 teaspoon vanilla
Chopped nuts

Combine all ingredients except nuts and beat until of spreading consistency. Spread frosting on cake, sprinkling nuts between layers and on top of cake.

Mrs. Malcolm Knight

Orange Chiffon Cake

1 angel food cake, cut into 3 layers
1 cup sugar
2 eggs
Juice of 1 orange

Juice and grated rind of 1 lemon
1 pint whipping cream, whipped

Combine sugar, eggs, orange juice, and lemon rind and juice. Boil until of custard consistency. Cool. Fold in whipped cream. Spread between layers and on top of cake. Keep refrigerated.

Frances Moore

Prune Nut Cake

2 cups self-rising flour	1 cup cream
2 cups sugar	3 eggs
1 teaspoon nutmeg	1 jar junior-size baby prunes
1 teaspoon allspice	1 cup black walnuts, chopped
1 cup cooking oil	

Sift dry ingredients. Add all other ingredients to dry ingredients and mix well. Pour batter into greased and floured tube pan and bake at 350 degrees for 1 hour.

Chris Bates

Short Fruit Cake

1 can condensed milk
3 cups shredded coconut
1 cup chopped pecans
1 cup chopped dates

Mix ingredients together. Line tube pan with wax paper. Bake 30 minutes at 375 degrees. Turn out and cool. Nice for cookies; bake 15 minutes at 350 degrees.

Ella Moore

Sour Cream Pound Cake

3 cups sugar	½ teaspoon soda
6 eggs	Pinch of salt
½ pound butter	1 teaspoon lemon extract
3 cups cake flour	1 teaspoon vanilla extract
1 (8-ounce) carton sour cream	

Cream butter and sugar; add eggs 1 at a time and beat after each egg. Add sour cream and extracts and mix well. Mix flour, salt, and soda and add to mixture. Stir batter until smooth. Bake in large tube pan which has been greased and floured lightly. Bake at 300 degrees for 1 hour and 30 minutes. (Check after 1 hour and 15 minutes). Keeps well up to a week.

Gell Richardson

Strawberry Cake

1 package white cake mix
1 cup oil
½ cup water
½ cup sugar
5 tablespoons flour
4 eggs
1 cup pecans, chopped
¾ package frozen strawberries, thawed
1 small package strawberry gelatin

Beat all ingredients together, blending well. Bake in greased and floured layer pans in preheated 325-degree over for 40 minutes.

Frosting:

1 stick butter or margarine, softened
¼ package frozen strawberries, thawed
1 box powdered sugar

Cream butter and sugar, adding enough strawberry juice for spreading consistency. Frost layers and top of cake and decorate with fresh berries, if desired.

Mrs. Malcolm Knight

White Fruit Cake

5 large eggs	¾ pound glacé cherries
½ pound butter	1 pound glacé pineapple
1 cup sugar	4 cups pecans
1¾ cups regular flour	½-ounce bottle vanilla flavoring
½ teaspoon baking powder	½-ounce bottle lemon flavoring

Cream butter and sugar well until fluffy. Add well beaten eggs and blend well. Chop nuts and fruit in medium pieces. Mix with part of flour. Sift remaining flour and baking powder together. Fold into egg and butter mixture. Add flavorings. Mix, then add fruit and nuts, mixing well. Pour into greased paper-lined tube pan. Place in cold over and bake at 250 degrees for 3 hours. Cool in pan on cake rack.

Mrs. Bill King
(from *Tampa Tribune*)

Angel Kisses

2 egg whites, stiffly beaten
⅔ cup sugar
Dash salt
1 teaspoon vanilla
1 cup pecan pieces
1 (6-ounce) package chocolate chips

Gradually add sugar to stiffly beaten egg whites. Add dash of salt. Fold in remaining ingredients. Drop by well-rounded teaspoonfuls onto greased cookie sheets. Place cookie sheets into preheated 350-degree oven. Turn oven off immediately. Leave cookies in oven overnight or until oven is cold. Good for teas, open houses, etc.

Mrs. Bill King
(from *Mrs. R. C. Calloway, Jr.*)

Boiled Cookies

1 stick margarine
2 cups sugar
4 tablespoons cocoa
½ cup milk
½ cup peanut butter
½ cup chopped pecans
2½ to 3 cups quick-cooking oatmeal

Combine margarine, sugar, cocoa, and milk in saucepan. Bring to boil and boil 1 minute. Stir in peanut butter, chopped pecans, and oatmeal. Drop by well-rounded teaspoonfuls onto wax paper and let cool.

Mrs. E. Clarence Shealy

Brownies

½ cup shortening	3 tablespoons cocoa
1 cup sugar	1 scant teaspoon salt
2 eggs	1 teaspoon vanilla
¾ cup flour	1 cup chopped nuts

Cream sugar and shortening. Add eggs. Sift dry ingredients and add to creamed mixture. Stir in vanilla and chopped nuts. Pour batter into greased and floured 8-by-8-inch square pan. Bake at 350 degrees for 25 minutes. Cut into squares while still warm.

Frances Moore

Chocolate Chip Cookies

2¼ cups flour
1 teaspoon baking soda
1 teaspoon salt
1 cup butter or margarine, softened
¾ cup sugar
¾ cup firmly packed brown sugar
1 teaspoon vanilla
½ teaspoon water
2 eggs
1 (12-ounce) package semisweet chocolate morsels
1 cup chopped nuts

Combine softened butter or margarine, sugar, brown sugar, vanilla, and water and beat until creamy. Sift flour, baking soda, and salt. Beat eggs into creamed mixture. Add dry ingredients; mix well. Stir in chocolate morsels and nuts. Drop onto greased cookie sheet by well-rounded teaspoonfuls. Bake at 375 degrees for 10 to 12 minutes. Makes about 100 cookies.

Mrs. Paul Hjort

Chocolate Meringues

3 egg whites
¼ teaspoon cream of tartar
Dash salt
1 teaspoon vanilla

1 cup sugar
1 (12-ounce) package chocolate chips

Beat egg whites until frothy adding cream of tartar, salt, and vanilla. Gradually add sugar until mixture is stiff. Stir in chocolate chips. Spoon onto greased cookie sheet. Bake approximately 1 hour at 250 degrees. Cool.

Betty Van Gerpen

Crescents

½ pound butter
5 heaping tablespoons confectioners' sugar
2 cups plain flour
1½ teaspoons vanilla
1 cup finely chopped nuts

Cream butter and sugar, add other ingredients. Break off small amount and roll into desired shape. Bake in slow oven until light brown. Cool and roll in confectioners' sugar.

Mrs. Paul Hjort

Fruit Cake Cookies

1 cup brown sugar
½ cup butter
4 eggs-separated
4 ounces milk
3 teaspoons soda dissolved in 3 tablespoons sour milk
1 pound dates
1 pound candied cherries
1 pound candied pineapple
6 cups shelled nuts
1 pound white raisins
1 teaspoon cinnamon
1 teaspoon nutmeg
3 cups flour, divided

Beat egg whites till stiff and set aside. Mix fruits and spices together and mix with 1 cup of the flour. Cream butter and sugar. Add milk, soda and milk mixture, egg yolks, and stir. Add the fruit and flour mixture and the rest of the flour (2 cups) and mix well. Fold in egg whites. Drop by rounded teaspoonfuls about 2 inches apart on greased baking sheet. Bake at 300 degrees for 20 minutes. Yield about 5 dozen.

Lealice Dehoney

Mrs. Donaldson's Ice Cream Cone Cake

1 box yellow cake mix
Ice cream cones, flat on botton
White, pink, or chocolate icing

Prepare cake batter as directed on box. Pour into cone, filling half full. Set cones in muffin tins to bake. Bake according to instructions for cupcakes. Ice as desired.

Melting Moments

⅔ cup unsifted cornstarch
⅓ cup unsifted powdered sugar
1 cup unsifted flour
1 cup butter (no substitutions)

Cream the butter and add powdered sugar. Sift flour and cornstarch together and add to butter mixture. Drop from teaspoon onto ungreased cookie sheet. Bake at 325 degrees for 10 to 12 minutes or just until firm. Do not brown.

Frosting:

⅓ cup soft butter
¼ box powdered sugar
3 tablespoons lemon juice
3 tablespoons grated lemon rind (use fresh lemon)

Beat all ingredients together in mixer. Spread on cooled cookies.

Betty Van Gerpen

Mincemeat Cookies

1 cup shortening
1 (9-ounce) package mincemeat
2 cups white sugar
4 whole eggs

4 cups flour
½ teaspoon cinnamon
¼ teaspoon allspice
1 teaspoon cloves
Pinch of salt
1 teaspoon soda
2 tablespoons boiling water

Cream shortening, mincemeat, sugar, and eggs. Sift together flour, cinnamon, allspice, cloves, and salt. Dissolve soda in boiling water. Mix all ingredients together well. Drop by teaspoonfuls onto greased cookie sheet. Bake at 375 degrees about 10 minutes.

Mrs. Grady Gatlin

Pecan Chews

2 eggs
2 cups brown sugar
10 rounded tablespoons flour
¼ teaspoon soda
1 cup nuts
1 teaspoon vanilla
2 tablespoons butter

Beat sugar and eggs until fluffy. Add flour, soda, and vanilla; fold in nuts. Melt butter in pan and pour batter over it. Bake 20 minutes at 350 degrees. Cut while warm.

Lealice Dehoney

Rice Cereal Marshmallow Treats

1 stick margarine
40 regular-size marshmallows or 4 cups miniature marshmallows
5 or 6 cups rice cereal
1 teaspoon vanilla

Melt in saucepan margarine and marshmallows, stirring constantly. Remove from heat, add vanilla, and stir in rice cereal until all grains are coated. Press evenly and firmly into buttered shallow pan. Cut into 2-inch squares when cool. These are easy to make.

Mrs. E. Clarence Shealy

S'mores

Saltines   **Marshmallows**
Peanut butter

Put saltines on cookie sheet. Spread crackers with peanut butter; place marshmallows on each square. Run under broiler until brown and marshmallow looks toasted. Serve immediately. Good, gooey—fast!

Carolyn Self

Spritz Cookies

2¼ cups sifted flour
½ teaspoon baking powder
¼ teaspoon salt
1 cup shortening (can use part butter)
¾ cup sugar
1 egg or 3 egg yolks beaten
1 teaspoon almond extract (or vanilla)

Sift together flour, baking powder, and salt. Cream shortening; add sugar and beat until light. Add egg and almond extract. Add dry ingredients; may need to mix with hands. Chill. Put dough through cookie press onto ungreased baking sheet. Sprinkle on decorative sugars. Bake in 400-degree oven for 7 to 10 minutes until set but not brown. Makes 6 dozen.

There is a certain twist of the wrist that makes the cookie form well. Practice until you get the trick under control. Use the same dough over and over until you get it right.

Chess Pie

1 stick margarine   1 tablespoon vinegar
1½ cups sugar   1 teaspoon vanilla
3 whole eggs   1 unbaked pie crust
1 tablespoon cornmeal

Melt margarine. Stir in sugar. Beat in eggs, cornmeal, vinegar, and vanilla. Pour into unbaked pie crust. Bake at 350 degrees for 45 minutes.

Lealice Dehoney via Mrs. Southerland's file

Chocolate Delight

Crust

1 cup flour   ½ cup nuts, finely chopped
1 stick margarine, softened

Second Layer

1 cup sifted powdered sugar
1 (8-ounce) package cream cheese, softened
½ large container whipped topping

Third Layer

2 packages instant chocolate pudding
3 cups milk

Fourth Layer

Remaining whipped topping   Chopped pecans

To make crust combine all ingredients until crumbly. Pat mixture into bottom of 13-by-9-inch pan (or 2-quart rectangular casserole). Bake at 300 degrees for 15 minutes. Cool. For second layer, combine powdered sugar and cream cheese and mix well. Add whipped topping and spread mixture over crust. Make third layer by combining pudding and milk and pour over second layer when pudding has set. Spread remaining whipped topping on top and sprinkle with chopped pecans.

Mrs. Malcolm Knight

Coquilles Venus

Pie pastry for 2-crust pie
3 pints firm, ripe strawberries
⅓ cup sugar
2 teaspoons brandy
1 cup red currant jelly
2 tablespoons brandy
Sweetened whipped cream flavored with brandy

Roll pastry dough to ⅛ inch thickness. Press dough into a scallop shell. Press second scallop shell lightly but firmly on top of the dough. Trim the dough to the edge of the shells and chill for 1 hour. Put the shells on a baking sheet and bake in the middle of a preheated 400-degree oven for 15 to 20 minutes, or until lightly colored. Remove scallop shells, transfer pastry to rack, and let cool. It takes two shells for each serving.

Hull and wash strawberries. In a large bowl, toss strawberries with sugar and 2 teaspoons of the brandy. In saucepan, combine red currant jelly with the 2 tablespoons of brandy; melt jelly over moderate heat and strain it into a small bowl. Brush the jelly glaze on the insides of the shells and fill them with strawberries. Top the berries with a generous amount of the sweetened whipped cream. Arrange a second shell over the whipped cream so that it looks like a half-opened scallop shell.

This is one of the prettiest desserts I know of. We keep the shells on hand and have also used them to hold other fruits and ice cream. They are quite impressive holding creamed tuna, lobster thermidor—you name it. You can't miss with this one.

Doty Bean

Fresh Fruit with Chocolate Meringues

3 egg whites
¼ teaspoon cream of tartar
Dash salt
1 teaspoon vanilla
1 cup sugar
1 (12-ounce) package chocolate chips
Fresh fruit

Beat egg whites until frothy, adding cream of tartar, salt, and vanilla. Gradually add sugar until mixture is stiff. Stir in chocolate chips. Spoon onto greased cookie sheet. Bake approximately 1 hour at 250 degrees. Cool. Serve with fresh fruit.

Betty Van Gerpen

Gelatin Pie

1 package lemon gelatin
1 package lime gelatin
1 package orange gelatin
1 package cherry or strawberry gelatin
½ cup pineapple juice
2 tablespoons sugar

2 cups whipped topping (nondairy or whipping cream)
4 cups hot water
1½ cups cold water

Mix lime gelatin with 1 cup hot water and ½ cup cold water. Chill until congealed in pan and then cut into cubes. Follow same procedure with orange and cherry gelatins. Mix lemon gelatin with 1 cup hot water, ½ cup pineapple juice, and 2 tablespoons sugar. Chill until slightly thickened, then blend in 2 cups whipped topping. Fold gelatin cubes into lemon gelatin mixture. Fill graham cracker pie crust or parfait glasses. Chill 5 hours or overnight. Serves 6.

Ella Moore

Lemon Chiffon Pie

1 envelope gelatin
2 tablespoons water
4 eggs, separated
½ cup lemon juice
¼ teaspoon salt
¾ cup sugar
1½ teaspoons grated lemon rind
1 (9-inch) baked pie crust

Soften gelatin in cold water. Beat egg yolks until light. Add lemon juice, salt, and ½ cup sugar. Cook in double boiler until thickened, stirring constantly. Add softened gelatin to hot mixture. Beat egg whites until stiff. Beat in remaining sugar and lemon rind. Fold into gelatin mixture. Pour into baked 9-inch pie crust.

Mrs. Tom Vann, Jr.

Lemon Pie

3 eggs, separated	1¼ cups water
1 cup sugar	3 tablespoons cornstarch
Rind of 1 large lemon	6 tablespoons sugar
Juice of 1½ large lemons	Yellow food coloring
Dash salt	1 (9-inch) baked pie shell

Mix cornstarch, sugar, water, and salt together and cook over low heat until transparent. Add lemon juice and rind to mixture and stir. Add egg yolks and stir. Add a few drops of yellow coloring. Let steam and stir for 4 or 5 minutes. Cover and cool. Whip egg whites until stiff, using 2 tablespoons of sugar for each egg white. Pour lemon mixture into baked pie shell. Cover with meringue. Bake in 325-degree oven until brown.

Mrs. E. Clarence Shealy

Million Dollar Pie

1 large container whipped topping
1 can sweetened condensed milk
1 (No. 2) can crushed pineapple, drained
5 tablespoons lemon juice, fresh or bottled
½ to 1 cup chopped pecans
1 small jar Maraschino cherries, chopped
2 prepared graham cracker crusts

Mix all ingredients and pour into shells. These may be well chilled, and served, or they may be frozen for later use. When freezing, turn the plastic liner upside down over pie and crimp edges for cover.

Wynelle MacMullen

Pickups

Crust:

1 (3-ounce) package cream cheese
1 stick butter or margarine
1 cup flour

Mix until smooth and chill. Pat small amounts into each cup of small muffin tins and press evenly around sides and bottom. (It's easiest to roll the chilled dough into slightly smaller-than-walnut balls before shaping into shells.)

Filling:

¾ cup dark brown sugar, packed firmly
1 teaspoon vanilla
1 tablespoon butter, melted
½ cup finely chopped pecans
1 egg

Mix all filling ingredients together well and put 1 teaspoonful into each pastry-lined cup. Bake at 350 degrees until crust is golden brown. Makes 24.

Mrs. E. Clarence Shealy

Quick and Easy Chocolate Pie

1 stick margarine
1½ squares unsweetened chocolate
1 cup sugar
2 eggs beaten
1 teaspoon vanilla
1 (9-inch) unbaked pie shell

Melt margarine and chocolate in saucepan. Remove from heat; add vanilla, eggs, and sugar. Mix well. Pour into unbaked pie shell and bake at 350 degrees for 30 minutes. Serve warm or cool with whipped cream or vanilla ice cream.

Mrs. E. Clarence Shealy

Zwieback Layer Pie or Pudding

2 cups milk
3 egg yolks, beaten
1 teaspoon vanilla
½ cup sugar
1 heaping tablespoon cornstarch
¼ teaspoon salt

Mix sugar, cornstarch, and salt. Add milk gradually and cook over low heat in saucepan or in double boiler until smooth and thickened. Add small amount of mixture to beaten egg yolks, return to mixture, and continue to cook over low heat until mixture reaches custard consistency. Add vanilla; cover while making meringue of egg whites and sugar. (Instant vanilla pudding may be substituted.)

Crust:

1 package zwieback, rolled
½ cup butter, melted
½ cup sugar

1 tablespoon cinnamon
½ teaspoon nutmeg

Meringue:

3 egg whites, beaten stiff   ⅓ cup sugar

Mix sugar, spices, and rolled zwieback together well before adding melted butter. Press one half of mixture into 9-inch pie plate. Reserve other half for upper crust. Make meringue. Pour custard into pie shell. Add meringue, then remainder of zwieback mixture. Bake at 350 degrees about 20 minutes or until brown.

Chocolate Chip Ice Cream

4 eggs
2½ cups sugar
1½ quarts milk
1 quart half-and-half
1½ tablespoons vanilla
½ teaspoon salt
1 (6-ounce) package chocolate chips, chilled

Beat eggs until light and fluffy, gradually adding sugar until thick and lemon colored. Beat in remaining ingredients and pour into freezer can. Add 6 ounces of chocolate chips that have been chilled to ice cream mixture after it has churned about 10 minutes.

Mr. and Mrs. Paul Hjort

Peppermint Ice Cream

4 eggs
2½ cups sugar
1½ quarts homogenized milk
1 quart light cream (may use half-and-half)
1½ teaspoons vanilla
½ teaspoon salt
1 large peppermint candy cane, crushed or two bags peppermint candy

Beat eggs until light and fluffy. Gradually add sugar, beating until thick and lemon colored. Beat in remaining ingredients and pour into freezer can. Freeze in electric or hand-turned churn. Makes 1 gallon. The candy with more red color gives the ice cream a deeper color. You may add a drop or two of red food coloring. (I crush candy in a bag with a hammer.) The crushed candy will dissolve in milk-egg mixture, and even if there are small chunks left, they're delicious in ice cream! You may have to let mixture sit in refrigerator awhile to let candy dissolve, but it freezes better if it's icy-cold when you start anyway!

Mrs. James R. Neill

Vanilla Ice Cream

4 large eggs
1 cup sugar
2 cups condensed milk
1½ quarts sweet milk (use little extra to rinse bowl and add to mixture)
1 tablespoon vanilla

Beat eggs well. Add sugar and mix thoroughly. Add condensed milk and continue mixing. Then add milk and vanilla. Pour into ice cream freezer. (May add peaches or bananas or strawberries for variation.)

Mrs. William King

Fruit Sherbet
(for 1 gallon freezer)

Juice of 3 lemons	2½ cups sugar
Juice of 3 oranges	1 large can evaporated milk
Small can pineapple juice	Whole milk

Mix all ingredients except whole milk. Pour in freezer and then add enough whole milk to fill the freezer ⅔ full. Some freezers have a fill line on them. Always leave space at top of freezer to allow for expansion. Freeze. Very light and fresh tasting.

Lealice Dehoney

Baked Custard

4 eggs	1 teaspoon salt
8 tablespoons sugar	1 teaspoon vanilla
4 cups milk	Nutmeg

Beat eggs; add salt, sugar, then milk and vanilla. Put into buttered baking cups. Sprinkle with nutmeg. Bake in pan of hot water for 45 minutes at 350 degrees. Serves 6.

Frances Moore

Pudding

1 cup sugar	⅛ teaspoon ground cloves
2 eggs	⅛ teaspoon ground nutmeg
2 cups finely chopped suet	1 teaspoon cinnamon
1 cup molasses	1 teaspoon baking powder
1 teaspoon salt	½ to 1 cup milk
1teaspoon soda	2 cups raisins
⅓ cup boiling water	1 cup currants
3½ cups flour	½ cup nutmeats (walnuts)

Dissolve soda in boiling water. Combine soda and water mixture with sugar, eggs, suet, molasses, and salt. Sift together flour, cloves, nutmeg, cinnamon, and baking powder. Add dry ingredients alternately with milk to first mixture. Add raisins, currants, and nutmeats. Fill mold two thirds full and steam for 2 hours.

Sauce for pudding:

1 stick butter	2 eggs, separated
2 cups sugar	3 tablespoons boiling water

Cream butter, sugar, and egg yolks. Add boiling water. Cook in top of double boiler until clear, stirring constantly. Beat egg whites until stiff. Pour cooked mixture over beaten egg whites and mix lightly. Serve over hot pudding at once. This is a traditional dessert at the Dehoney house at Christmas.

Lealice Dehoney

Grape-Nuts Pudding

1 teaspoon grated lemon rind
4 tablespoons butter or margarine
1 cup sugar
2 egg yolks, well beaten
3 tablespoons lemon juice
2 tablespoons flour

4 tablespoons Grape-Nuts flakes
1 cup milk
2 egg whites, stiffly beaten

Cream butter and lemon rind; add sugar gradually. Add egg yolks, beat thoroughly. Add lemon juice, then flour, Grape-Nuts flakes and milk. Mix well. Fold in egg whites. Turn into buttered pan 8-by-8-inches. Place in pan of hot water. Bake at 325 degrees in preheated oven for 1 hour and 15 minutes. A crust will form on top and custard below when it is done. Serves 4 generously.

Frances Moore

Fresh Strawberry Mousse

1 pint fresh strawberries
2 (3-ounce) packages strawberry gelatin
¼ cup sugar
1 pint whipping cream

Crush strawberries and drain. Reserve juice. Add enough water to juice to make 1½ cups liquid. Bring this liquid to a boil; stir in gelatin, dissolve, and cool. Add strawberries and sugar. Whip cream until it stands in tall peaks. Fold into strawberry mixture. Pour into 2-quart mold. Chill several hours or overnight. Serves 8 to 10.

Substitutions: Instead of fresh fruit use 2 (10-ounce) packages of frozen strawberries and *omit* sugar. Substitute nondairy whipped topping for whipping cream.

Ella Moore

Spanish Caramelized Custard

Caramelize 1 cup granulated sugar, using this method: Place sugar in a heavy pan over very low heat. Add 1 tablespoon water and stir constantly with long handled wooden spoon for about 8 to 10 minutes until sugar is melted and turns a light brown color. Remove pan from heat. *Very slowly* and carefully add ¼ cup very hot water. Care is necessary to make the syrup smooth. Return the pan to low heat and stir continuously for another 8 to 10 minutes until the mixture is the color of maple syrup.

Now place the caramelized sugar in a 7-inch ring mold or in 6 custard cups. (If you have too much syrup, put it in a small jar and keep it in the refrigerator for a later time.) Turn the mold to allow the caramel to spread evenly. The syrup should be thick.

Custard:

2 cups milk
Grated rind of 1 lime (optional)
1 teaspoon grated cinnamon
3 egg whites
¾ cup sugar
½ teaspoon grated nutmeg
¼ teaspoon salt
6 egg yolks
1 teaspoon vanilla

Preheat oven to 325 degrees. Place all ingredients in blender (or deep mixing bowl and beat with electric beaters). Blend at high speed. Pour into mold or cups on top of caramel. Place mold or cups in a pan containing an inch of hot (not boiling) water. Bake in 325-degree oven for about an hour. Test at 45 minutes by inserting a knife near the edge of the cup. If the blade comes out clean, remove the custard from the pan and cool. When completely cooled, invert it onto a platter. To be sure the caramel comes out evenly, dip the mold up to the caramel level in hot water very quickly. Fill center of mold (or serve each cup) with whipped cream sprinkled with slivered toasted almonds or coconut. Serves 6.

Mrs. Rafael Reyes

Milk Chocolate Fondue

2 (8-ounce) packages milk chocolate squares
1 cup cream
Few drops peppermint flavoring or crème de menthe (optional)

Grate chocolate and place in fondue pot with cream. Stir well and heat gently, stirring until chocolate is melted. Add flavoring. Be careful to keep heat on very low to avoid scorching. Serves 8.

Carolyn Self

Mocha Fondue

2 (8-ounce) packages milk chocolate squares
2 tablespoons instant coffee powder
1½ cups cream

Grate chocolate and mix with coffee powder. Place in a fondue pot with cream. Stir over low heat until chocolate is melted. Add a few drops of grenadine or crème de menthe if desired. Serves 8.

Carolyn Self

Lemon Dessert

Crust:

½ stick margarine
3 tablespoons sugar
1¼ cups crushed graham crackers (12 to 15 crackers)

Mix these ingredients together well and press into a greased 11½ by 8 inch casserole. Save about ¼ cup of crumb mixture to sprinkle on top of pie.

Filling:

1 (8-ounce) package cream cheese
1 cup sugar
1 teaspoon vanilla
1 (3-ounce) package lemon gelatin
1 cup hot water
1 can evaporated milk (iced)

Cream together the cream cheese, sugar, and vanilla in a large mixing bowl. In a small bowl dissolve the gelatin in the hot water. Let this cool completely (bowl can be set in a pan of ice). Add gelatin to cream cheese mixture. Add the iced can of evaporated milk (the milk must be chunky with ice), and beat at high speed of mixer. Pour into crust and sprinkle with remaining crumb mixture. Refrigerate for 3 or 4 hours before serving. The icier the milk, the higher the dessert.

Anne King

Punch

Banana Punch

6 cups water
3 cups pineapple juice
Juice of two lemons
3 or 4 bananas, pureed in blender
3¼ cups sugar
2 (6-ounce) cans frozen orange juice
3 large bottles ginger ale
Food coloring (optional)

Mix together all ingredients except ginger ale. Freeze for 24 hours, taking out an hour before serving. Mash with potato masher until a slush consistency in punch bowl. Add ice cold ginger ale and serve. Color may be added. Serves 36.

Mrs. Malcolm Knight

Coffee Mocha

1 gallon boiling water
1 cup instant coffee
3 squares semisweet chocolate
2 tablespoons vanilla
1 cup sugar
2 quarts milk
1 gallon ice cream (chocolate or vanilla)

Mix first 5 ingredients and chill overnight. When ready to serve, add milk and ice cream. Serves 50.

Mrs. Huddie Cheney

Easy Punch
(Hawaiian)

1 large can fruit punch
½ bottle ginger ale
1 small can lemonade concentrate (undiluted)

Mix all ingredients and refrigerate for several hours before using.

Carolyn Self

Easy Punch
(Pineapple)

1 large can pineapple juice   1 box thawed strawberries
1 large bottle ginger ale

Freeze can of pineapple juice, then thaw so it will be slushy in the punch bowl. Add ginger ale and strawberries.

Carolyn Self

Fresh and Easy Punch

2 pints pineapple sherbet
2 bottles Wink grapefruit drink

Place sherbert in punch bowl. Add grapefruit drink. Stir to mix. Makes about 24 servings.

Lealice Dehoney

Iced Coffee Special

Serve iced coffee with a topping of whipped cream flavored with one of the following: grated orange or lemon rind, grated chocolate, chocolate syrup, cocoa, cinnamon, nutmeg, almond extract, mint extract, or vanilla extract.

Instant Hot Chocolate Mix
(Makes mountains of cups)

1 (32-ounce) box Nestlé's Quick
1 (8-quart) box powdered milk
1 (16-ounce) jar Carnation Coffeemate

Mix well. Fill cup one third to one half full and add boiling water.

Mrs. Bill King
Mrs. John King, Jr.
Mrs. Randolph Malone

Mulled Cider

1 gallon apple cider	Allspice
1 (46-ounce) can orange juice	Cinnamon sticks
1 small can frozen lemonade	Grated nutmeg
Whole cloves	

Heat first 3 ingredients. Add spices tied in a piece of cloth. Let simmer until you achieve desired flavor.

Mrs. Bill King

Red Party Punch

4 quarts water
3 cups sugar
2 (6-ounce) cans frozen lemon juice
2 quarts cranberry juice
1 quart apple juice
1 pint orange juice
1 pint tea

Mix water and sugar; bring to boil. Combine with rest of ingredients. Mix well. Chill before using. Makes 2 gallons or 40 servings.

Wynelle MacMullen

Quick Coffee Punch

1 (2-ounce) jar instant coffee
12 cups boiling water
8 cups cool water
½ gallon chocolate ice cream
½ gallon vanilla ice cream

Mix instant coffee with boiling water. Add cool water. Just before serving, add the ice cream. Serves 30 to 40 people.

Dot Harris
Jane Guthrie

Spiced Tea

1 (1-pound, 2-ounce) jar Tang | 1 teaspoon ground cinnamon
1¼ cups sugar | ½ teaspoon ground cloves
¾ cup instant tea | Dash salt

Mix all ingredients. Use one heaping teaspoon of mix for each cup of hot water.

Ella Moore

Summer Cooler

Instant coffee
Boiling water
Crushed ice
Vanilla, coffee, or chocolate ice cream

For each serving, pour 1 cup boiling water over 1 teaspoon instant coffee. Stir. Half fill a tall glass with crushed ice. Add 2 scoops of ice cream. Add hot coffee and stir. Serve with straws and a spoon.

Teate Punch

1 (46-ounce) can pineapple juice
1 large can frozen lemonade
1 lemonade can of water
Food coloring (optional)

Mix all ingredients. This makes a little over two quarts. You should double this for 1 gallon, which would serve 32 cups.

Barbara Nunnally

Tomato Juice Cocktail

1 large can tomato juice
¼ can lemon juice
1 teaspoon sugar
¼ teaspoon onion powder
2 teaspoons Worcestershire sauce
2 teaspoons prepared horseradish sauce
Salt to taste

Mix well, chill, and serve.

Ella Moore

Viennese Coffee Punch

Instant coffee
4 crushed cinnamon sticks
8 whole cloves
8 allspice berries

2 tablespoons sugar
1 quart boiling water
Sweetened whipped cream
Cinnamon sticks for garnish

Using 2 teaspoons instant coffee for each cup water, make coffee cubes or ring by pouring mixture into refrigerator tray or a 9-inch ring mold. Pour 1 quart boiling water over 2 table-spoons instant coffee, crushed cinnamon sticks, cloves, allspice, and sugar. Chill at least 1 hour. To serve, strain into punch bowl. Add coffee cubes or ring. Ladle into glasses or mugs. Accompany with sweetened whipped cream and a cinnamon stick per serving. Dollops of whipped cream can be placed around punch bowl.

Christmas or New Year's Wassail

6 (1-inch) cinnamon sticks
16 whole cloves
1 teaspoon whole allspice
3 medium oranges
6 cups apple cider or apple juice
2 cups cranberry cocktail juice
¼ cup sugar
1 teaspoon aromatic bitters

Break cinnamon in 1-inch pieces and tie with cloves and allspice in cheesecloth bag. Stud oranges with additional whole cloves. In large saucepan combine cider, cranberry juice, sugar, bitters, spice bag and whole oranges. Cover and simmer ten minutes. Remove spice bag and oranges. Pour into warm bowl. Float oranges. Add additional orange slices. Serves 20.

Ella Moore

Wassail Bowl

3 large cooking apples, cored and sliced crosswise
2 oranges sliced crosswise and pierced with cloves on skin surface
1 gallon apple cider

6 whole cloves
6 whole allspice
2 teaspoons nutmeg
1 (6-ounce) can frozen lemonade, undiluted
1 (6-ounce) can frozen orange juice, undiluted
1 cup brown sugar.

About 45 minutes before serving, bake apples about 25 minutes in 350-degree oven. Over low heat simmer 2 cups cider, allspice, nutmeg, and cloves for 10 minutes. Add remaining cider, orange juice, lemonade, and brown sugar. Heat, but do not boil. Float apple and orange slices and serve hot. Makes 36 half-cup servings.

Nancy Simmons

Random Notes

1. Ideally no meal should contain more than one rich dish.

2. If you have cream soup, try not to serve another dish with cream in it.

3. A lettuce leaf placed in a pot of soup will absorb the grease (discard leaf).

4. To make delicious salad dressing, mix mayonnaise, ketchup, and pickle juice together to proper consistency.

5. A little almond flavoring makes lots of things (cakes, cookies, icings) taste special.

6. Never choose a creamy dessert if meal has a cream sauce dish.

7. Make dessert portions small. Dieters will not feel so bad if they indulge.

8. Never use fewer than four candles on the table—use candles only after six o'clock.

9. For quick soups try combinations of canned soups, such as cream of tomato and cream of mushroom or cream of celery—use your imagination.

10. Sour cream and lemon pepper added to scrambled eggs makes them light, fluffy, and delicious! Use a whisk to blend.

11. For low sodium–low fat cooking use salt-free bouillon cubes for flavor and seasoning. Chicken bouillon goes well with most vegetables and of course with chicken and turkey.

12. To any fruit punch add 3 or 4 bananas (in blender). Delicious addition!

13. When seating guests at several tables, the host and hostess should sit at separate tables. Be sure to have an extrovert at the other tables. If you are all at one table, the host and hostess should sit opposite each other: she with male guest of honor at her right, he with female guest of honor at his right unless to keep the men and women alternated the hostess should be seated just around the corner if the table is oblong. This would place the male guest of honor opposite the host with the hostess to the right of the honored male guest.

Place cards help avoid confusion, and it's nice to put the first name of the person in large letters on the back of the place card for the benefit of those seated across the table.

14. Prepare and freeze a supply of spaghetti sauce which may be used as a basis for a bowl of chili on a cold winter evening. Add a can or two of beans and chili seasoning. Or use the sauce for Sloppy Joes for a crowd of hungry young people or the ever-popular spaghetti supper.

Substitutions

1. 1 cup cake flour equals 1 cup minus 2 tablespoons all-purpose flour.

2. 1 tablespoon cornstarch for thickening equals 2 tablespoons flour or 4 teaspoons quick-cooking tapioca.

3. 1 cup sour milk or buttermilk equals 1 tablespoon lemon juice or vinegar plus sweet milk to make 1 cup (let stand 5 minutes).

4. 1 tablespoon equals 3 teaspoons.

5. 1 teaspoon baking powder equals ¼ teaspoon soda plus ½ teaspoon cream of tartar.

6. Gelatin can be used instead of eggs in croquettes and such.

Things to Accumulate

1. Petite muffin tins—good for muffins for parties, miniature pies, etc.

2. All sorts and sizes of trays.

3. Pitchers: crystal, pottery.

4. Straw baskets (all sizes).

5. Small galvanized pails.

6. Wooden dough boards.

7. Cheese boards and slicers.

8. Candle holders (large variety—tall and short).

9. Cloth napkins: all sizes, various colors.

10. Casual table cloths and coordinating napkins.

11. Material for liners (baskets and pails).

12. A double boiler.

13. Electric fondue pots.

14. Glass ovenproof dishes and holders (some with candle or wick warmers).

15. Wire whisk.

16. Lots of wooden spoons, spatulas.

17. Cake/pie servers.

18. Pretty salt and pepper shakers.

19. Place cards.

20. Candles for emergencies and instant decoration.

21. Kerosene lamps for patio or outdoor use.

Index